DRIVING IN COMPETITION

DRIVING IN COMPETITION

ALAN JOHNSON

W • W • Norton & Company
New York • London

ISBN 0-393-60011-4

Library of Congress Card No. 73-81321

W. W. Norton & Company, Inc., 500 Fifth Avenue, New York, N.Y. 10110

Printed in the United States of America

4   5   6   7   8   9   0

Contents

Foreword

IF YOU'RE LOOKING for a book that is going to tell you how to become the World Champion Driver next year, then you might as well put this down right now. This isn't it. But if you're interested in road racing and want a practical book about the fundamentals of sports car racing in the United States, then this is a book that will interest you. It begins at the beginning, contains practical information on the pitfalls as well as the possible rewards in American club racing, and takes you step by step through the process of becoming a competition driver.

Alan Johnson is uniquely qualified to write such a book as this. He has been the whole route in SCCA club racing, regarding himself not as an extraordinarily gifted sportsman/athlete but as a more-or-less Joe Average Guy who started at the very beginning and has gone through the complete process. When I first knew Alan he was driving a street roadster, not a sports car, and was only circling around the edges of sports car racing, wondering whether this was what he really wanted to do. Before actually beginning his racing career, he thought about it for a long time, participating in California Sports Car Club activities in a variety of non-essential jobs, talking, watching, listening and learning about the sport. When he got his first sports car, a Porsche Speedster, he began his competition career as the purest kind of novice, going through the Cal Club's driver training program one small step at a time, just like almost every other driver in American club racing. He bought his own car, he prepared it himself and every nickel that went into his racing was his own. Since those early days when he was serving his apprenticeship back in the pack as owner/driver/mechanic/sponsor he has progressed through club racing to his current position as a 4-time SCCA National champion who is nationally known and nationally respected.

During his years in the sport he has paid his dues in many ways. He worked in the Cal Club's driver training program, spent his time as the club's chief instructor and has also served as Director of the Sports Car Club of America's Driver Licensing and Training program. In every page of this book it is evident that he has thought a lot about racing, analyzing not only what is done but why it is done, and has strived to find ways of describing the processes of competition driving in ways that will be meaningful to other drivers. Frankly, I wouldn't describe Alan as being a "natural" driver who instinctively knew what to do the first time he sat in a racing car—and for the purposes of this book, I think this is good. I think he had to *learn* to be a competition driver, to think about it, study every situation so that he became aware of the actual processes involved. And because he has done this, he is able to present it in a way that is most meaningful to other drivers.

About this book he has said, "What I tried to do is write a book that I would want to read if I were just starting in competition driving."

And in this I think he has succeeded very well.

—James T. Crow
Newport Beach, Calif.

What it Takes

THE CLASSIC QUALITIES that are usually listed as being
essential for a competition driver are these—lightning-like
reflexes, superb physical condition, tremendous courage,
and an overwhelming desire to win. Frankly, these things sound
to me like generalizations made by somebody who didn't know
very much about the subject. Admittedly, it does help if you
have good reflexes and don't freeze when faced with the
unexpected. Certainly, you do have to have a certain amount of
courage, if that's what it's called when you are able to control
your doubts and fears. And, of course, the better physical

condition you're in and the more you want to win, probably, the better are your chances of doing well. But as far as these qualities being required in any super-special amounts before you should consider driving in competition, I think they have been greatly over-emphasized.

Let's think about them. First, let's take lightning-like reflexes and other physical traits that imply that you have to be some sort of superman to be a competition driver. It is obvious that these qualities are of benefit to the person who wants to become a competition driver. But it doesn't mean that you have to have the coordination of a juggler or reflexes like a computer in order to be a racing car driver. There have been very good drivers with serious physical handicaps. Archie Scott-Brown, an English sports car racer, had a withered arm. Chet Miller and Pete Wood, who raced in the United States a few years ago, were extremely competitive with artificial legs. We had a local driver in Southern California, Tom Denner, who, although spastic, was able to qualify for an SCCA National competition license and derive a great deal of pleasure from driving in competition. It's true that no one, so far as I know, who has had a serious physical handicap has become a World Champion—I expect that you can't be much less than physically superb to be a World Champion—but many, many drivers who were a lot less than perfect physical specimens have raced and raced very well.

It is advantageous, obviously, to have good eyesight. The best drivers are alleged to have vision that is almost unreal. My own sight is better than 20/20 and I have always considered it an advantage. But a good many successful drivers have had not only less than perfect eyesight but there have been several who could see out of only one eye. Competition driving doesn't automatically exclude anyone who doesn't have super vision and if your eyesight can be corrected to something near normal through the use of glasses, there's no reason for your eyes to keep you from being a competition driver.

Neither is there any real limit on the age you have to be to drive in competition. Perhaps, like having a great physical condition and eyesight, if you plan to be a World Champion, you had better start young. But even if you don't, there's still no reason why you can't drive in competition and be pretty good at it. In SCCA at the present time you can start at 18 on the club-racing level although you must be 21 to drive in any of the professional series (Can-Am, etc.). Some organizations, such as the International Motor Sports Association, are also accepting 18-year-olds in their events. And there's certainly no limit on

Too old to race? Chuck Parsons (left), Jack Brabham (above) and Juan Manuel Fangio were as good as ever in their forties.

being too old. A lot of men who couldn't afford to race when they were in their twenties and thirties have gotten tremendous pleasure out of racing in their forties, fifties, and even in their sixties. My favorite example is Jack Hinkle of Wichita, Kansas, who is now in his mid-sixties yet drives and wins in the fastest and most competitive sports cars in SCCA club racing.

As for the second trait, having to have tremendous courage in order to drive in competition, I'd say this is overrated too. It's an admirable quality, to be sure, but any activity that involves physical risk requires a certain amount of courage. Just getting into your car and driving on the freeway requires some courage. In competition driving, as in driving on the freeway, you don't deliberately expose yourself to danger. You drive in such a way as to avoid taking unnecessary chances and you try to prepare yourself for any emergency that may arise. And you

11

also equip yourself with safety equipment in order to minimize the consequences of anything that may happen. You study the circumstances and you don't deliberately tempt fate. Personally, the thought of jumping out of an airplane scares me, and I have absolutely no desire to do it. My feelings might change, however, if I were to learn more about sky diving. I've had people involved in sports that I consider to be very dangerous tell me they sure wouldn't want to do what I do, and this always surprises me. I know what I'm doing and I feel security in knowing just what the risks are. In sports car racing, if you take the time to learn the sport, I believe you'll find that the risks are a lot lower than they appear to be to an outsider.

Far more important than raw courage of the kind that leads supposedly brave men to take chances with their lives is an ability to control the emotions, to *not* yield to the temptation to take a chance when you don't know what is going to happen. As far as competition driving is concerned, a driver is better off being a little bit cautious than being too brave.

So far as an overwhelming will to win is concerned, I think this is even more overrated than the other two. When I first started racing, for instance, I distinctly remember that I did *not* have anything like an overwhelming desire to win. When I went racing, what I really wanted to do was simply get out on the race track and work up to going as fast as I thought I could. To me, just being out there, being any kind of race driver, carried one whale of a lot of glamour at that time. It was a pretty big thing for me just to have a competition license and a car that had a rollbar and numbers. And when you think about it, simply being able to get a competition license is a worthwhile accomplishment even if you never win a trophy or get your name in the papers.

The desire to win may come later. I'd been racing for three years before I really felt that particular urge. This happened during a race at Del Mar, California, in 1963. I got into the lead early in the race and then Denny Harrison, driving another car like mine, passed me and went off about three to five seconds ahead. This was a 45-minute race and we stayed like that for perhaps 15 laps. Initially, I was quite content to stay in 2nd place and had no real compulsion to try to repass him. But as I watched him stay about the same distance ahead, not pulling any further away, I asked myself, "Why don't I get to work a little bit and see if I can catch him?" So I did. And by driving a little harder, concentrating a little more and trying as much as I could, I found that I was able to gain on him. I closed up right on his tail and pretty soon I could see that he was beginning to feel the pressure and was making little mistakes. Seeing this, I realized that if I waited for my opportunity and stayed cool, I was going to be able to get by him. And sure enough, I did get by and win the race.

I had begun to learn two very big things in racing—concentration and persistence—and I was further able to enjoy a feeling of accomplishment. I won't try to kid you—getting to the checkered flag first, especially when you know the competition has been good and you have used your talents, is tremendously satisfying; but for some, the emphasis on winning may be too great. Dave Pearson, the NASCAR Grand National Champion, when asked how he liked taking second in a major race, was quoted as saying, "Second place is just a little better than third." For the most part, I believe that this point of view is common to those racing car drivers who have become accustomed to winning. In recent years, I have won races that have not been satisfying for me because the competition wasn't there. And I have lost races that gave me a great deal of satisfaction because I knew I'd driven well.

The real point is that not every driver has to win races or even have a terrific desire to win to get a tremendous amount of pleasure out of racing. For many drivers, learning about racing, competing, and overcoming their own doubts about courage and ability afford a great amount of satisfaction and offer sufficient justification for becoming a competition driver.

The First Steps

T HE FIRST LOGICAL STEP to take in learning more about any subject is to expose yourself to all possible knowledge about it. This is certainly true about road racing. Presumably, since you're reading this book, you are interested in the subject and presumably you've seen at least a road race or two. This is important, of course, but there are also other things you can do before you get into a racing car for the first time.

First of all, you can read about racing. We're extremely fortunate that there have been several highly perceptive things that have been published about racing. There are two books that are worthwhile reading for anyone who is interested in the subject and these will give you more insight to competition driving than any others. The first of these is Piero Taruffi's *The Technique of Motor Racing.* Taruffi was a champion class driver in the late '40s and early '50s and has since that time operated his own driving school in Italy and has done much to educate many beginning drivers. The second book is *The Racing Driver* by Denis Jenkinson. Jenkinson is not himself a racing car driver but he is one of the most respected motoring journalists in the world and is a careful student of the art of driving. He was a motorcycle racer when he was young, he rode as passenger for Eric Oliver in championship class side-hack racing in Europe and he was with Stirling Moss as navigator in the classic Mille Miglia in 1955 when Moss won that race in one of the legendary Mercedes-Benz 300SLR sports cars. What Jenkinson has to tell you about racing drivers is worth knowing. These books may not, in every respect, be directly applicable to your own career as a race car driver but they are good background and present you with a lot to think about.

There are also many biographies of great drivers that have been published in the past few years. Unfortunately, most of these concentrate on the exciting events in their careers rather than on the techniques that made them great and consequently few of them are more than entertainment. They are interesting, though, because they do tell you something about how other drivers got their starts and what paths their careers took as they made their way to the top. Some of those that I have enjoyed include Bruce McLaren's *From the Cockpit,* Graham Hill's *Life at the Limit* and *Jim Clark, Portrait of a Great Driver,* edited by Graham Gauld. Also entertaining, although somewhat melodramatic, is the book that Stirling Moss wrote with Ken Purdy, *All But My Life.*

The weekly and monthly publications that cover racing are important to your background as well. Essential, I think, for keeping up with what's going on in U.S. road racing is *Autoweek* and a subscription to it is something I wouldn't be without. If you're especially interested in European racing and want more detail about these events than *Autoweek* gives you, then a subscription to *Motoring News* or *Autosport*, which are published in England, will give you this. The monthly magazines in the U.S. seem to be covering a smaller and smaller number of races but certainly *Road & Track* shouldn't be missed as long as Rob Walker's reports on the Grand Prix races appear there. Walker has a remarkable insight into racing because of his long participation in the sport as an entrant and independent team manager. The monthly publications also give you more in the way of technical information about race cars, race courses, etc.

You should also begin to learn the technicalities of road racing, the jargon, organization, rules, etc., by becoming familiar with the publication of the club you're going to race with. In fact, one of the first things you should do on becoming interested in road racing is to join a club if for no other reason than to get the literature they have available. Top priority among SCCA publications is the *General Competition Rules,* commonly called the GCR, a small book that is the bible of SCCA racing. In it are the regulations governing the preparation of cars, safety rules, car classifications, the general regulations for the conduct of SCCA events and much more. Another small book updated yearly is the *Production Car Specifications* which lists the specs for each car that SCCA has accepted for production car racing. These books are available from SCCA headquarters. The SCCA's monthly magazine, *Sports Car,* is also essential since that's where the new regulations and changes in regulations first appear officially. The International Motor Sports Association rule book, called the *IMSA Code,* is much less detailed than SCCA's GCR, but it's equally essential if you're going to be racing with IMSA. For international rules, you need the *FIA Yearbook of Automobile Sport.*

As a part of your general education in the sport, you should get just as completely involved as you can. If you know someone who is racing a car, you should try to get involved in helping him. If you don't know such a person, you may be able to locate one through a sports car dealer or an independent garage that specializes in sports cars. Spend your evenings in his garage, seeing what is required to prepare a car. Go with him to tech inspection and find out what goes on there; it will be an advantage for you to learn the workings of this segment of the club's organization. Tech inspection crews vary like race courses, and learning to deal with them is something that will ease the strain on your nerves when you go racing yourself. If your friend can get you a pit pass, fine. But even if he can't because his regular crew has already taken all the passes for his entry, maybe he'll allow you to buy an additional pass, which is usually possible, so you can go and observe the race from the pits and see just what goes on there. This is all volunteer, unpaid work, you understand, and for this reason many independent club racers are often glad to have you around as an extra hand that can be depended upon even if you are not an expert.

17

Another approach you might take is to become involved with the club that stages the road races in your area. Pay your membership dues, become a card-carrying member, go to the meetings, and volunteer for whatever jobs need to be done. But you should try to stay away from crowd control assignments as these usually place you away from the action and the kind of exposure you should have to get ready to go racing. If you are able to swing it, work on a corner crew. But even if you can't be intimately involved with the presentation of the races, there are still lots of jobs on inspection crews, emergency crews, pre-grid, scoring, timing, pit marshaling, etc., that are seldom overstaffed for minor events. You may even find that this kind of participation is so enjoyable in itself that you don't have to actually become a driver to have road racing become a pleasant and worthwhile hobby.

Becoming involved with the club's activities will also enable you to get acquainted with the officials in the club, to find out what their duties are and get to know who really knows the ins and outs of the sport. This can be a distinct advantage later

when you want to know something more about the regulations governing the drivers or the interpretation of the rules as they affect the preparation of the car.

If you already have a car, you can enter other types of competition—rallies, slaloms, gymkhanas, time trials, hillclimbs, and so on. These events don't require the expensive special equipment and special training, and therefore don't demand the same kind of financial investment as all-out road racing. Even in a slalom or autocross, you can apply the driving techniques that are described in this book and sharpen your skills ahead of time. It's excellent training.

And certainly you can apply many of the essentials of competition driving when you are driving your car on the street. At first glance it doesn't seem that this can be done but I think driving on the street is probably the most underrated place for learning and perfecting many of the essentials of competition driving. This doesn't mean that you have to be traveling at racing speeds but you can constantly practice the smoothness of competition driving, the essential concentration on what you're doing and the precise control that is also mandatory in racing.

Also, try to be sure that this is what you really want to do before you make the investment. I've seen it happen where the driver will go to the expense of getting just the right car, buy all the best safety gear, and spend all the money necessary to get his car prepared to the limit only to discover after his first time on a race track that he doesn't really want to be a racing driver. An amazingly large number of first-time students entering the SCCA's driver training program never come back a second time. This figure approaches 40 percent, which is a fantastically high drop-out rate. So try to hold your expenses to a minimum until you're absolutely certain that this is the sport for you.

Unfortunately, there's little likelihood that somebody else is going to furnish a car for you to find this out. Perhaps you could persuade a friend to lend or rent you his race-prepared car for this purpose but it isn't very likely even though you swear you'll pay him for it if you bend it. In some areas there are schools where you can rent cars for training purposes. The *IMSA Yearbook* lists those that are recognized for licensing purposes by IMSA and there are others that advertise in *Autoweek* from time to time. It's expensive to do it this way, as you would expect. The cost ranges from a minimum of about $50 up to $200 or more a day for the use of one of their cars. Nevertheless, this may be worth it to you if you think you want to drive in competition but aren't absolutely sure that you'll want to continue once you've tried it.

It is also extremely important before you actually start racing to make sure that you can honestly afford to go racing. It's expensive. Unbelievably expensive. So plan your expenditures just as carefully as you can. Many times I've seen people buy a race car and find themselves so overstretched financially that they can't even get to the track. It is much better—and a lot more fun—to start out with something you know you can afford, even if it doesn't have the class and glamour, than have this happen to you. So set your sights a little lower until you find out just how it is all going to work and how much it is really going to cost.

After you've added up your racing budget for your first season, taking into account preparing the car, buying safety equipment, paying entry fees and allowing for travel expenses, I'd suggest that you add about 50 percent to that total to come up with a realistic figure. You never know what's going to happen in racing. You don't know what new equipment is going to become available, you won't know just how long your tires are

20

going to last and you won't allow enough for the unexpected. If your car gets bent during a race, you are the one who has to stand the expense. No matter whose fault it is, no matter how innocent you are, you and nobody else will have to pay to repair it. So until you know through experience what your expenses will be, leave a sizable reserve for the unexpected.

When I first started racing, for example, I very quickly ran out of money. In no time at all I didn't have money for new tires. I remember actually starting a race with a tire nearly into the cords and because we moved it to the inside front where it didn't get much wear, I was able to finish the race. That kind of thing wouldn't happen today, because it would almost certainly be spotted by an official and you'd be ordered off the track. I can also remember blowing an engine in the latter part of 1961 and not being able to race again until the summer of 1962 simply because I didn't have the funds to get the engine back together. I've seen people roll their cars into a ball and simply have to leave racing permanently because of the financial bind it put them in.

So if you haven't planned your expenses very carefully, road racing can become a very sad experience. But if you plan carefully and go racing with an understanding of what it will cost and are financially prepared for the worst to happen, it can be a lot of fun...even if you have bad luck.

Mixed practice shows wide variety of cars used in club racing.

What Kind of Car?

THERE ARE MANY KINDS of automobiles being raced in this country—dragsters, midgets, sprints, USAC championship cars, stock cars, sports cars, dune buggies, karts, quarter midgets and so on. But for the purposes of this book, I'm going to assume you're interested in road racing cars. But even within the framework of road racing, there is a great variety. There are cars with the engine in the front, in the middle and in the rear. There are production category sports cars that vary from bug-eyed Sprites to 494-cubic-inch Sting Rays and there are pure racing cars that vary from relatively inexpensive to impossibly expensive. In addition, there are sedans that range from the Showroom Stock class all the way up to Trans-Am and IMSA sedans. So what kind of car should you race?

Let me start by saying again that road racing is expensive. I've said that before and I'll say it again before we're done. So you might as well get accustomed to that fact early in your career. The very cheapest kind of road racing at the present time is undoubtedly SCCA's "Showroom Stock" class. You have to put in an SCCA rollbar, you have to have the standard safety gear such as helmet, suit, harness and fire extinguisher, but except for allowing the use of any tire that is the same size as comes standard on the car, there are no modifications permitted. So you can get into racing for little more investment than one of these moderately priced sedans plus maybe $500 for the safety equipment and a set of radial tires. Assuming you don't roll it up in a ball, you could probably campaign a Showroom Stock for a full season for only a few hundred dollars, excluding the original investment, of course.

Admittedly, there isn't much glamour in racing a Showroom Stocker. Formula Vee is probably the next step up the price ladder. If you were to buy a used Vee in good condition, run a moderately stock engine, use a fairly hard rubber compound on your tires and drive with a certain amount of restraint, you could probably make it through a season for as little as it would cost to run a Showroom Stock sedan. A Vee doesn't offer the possibility of being used for everyday transportation, however, so your overall investment would be considerably greater.

No matter what you race, the price goes up depending on the number of races you run and how far you have to travel to the events. Even if you do the whole weekend on a budget there are motel bills, food, drink and gasoline to be considered. Also, if you want to have a chance to run at the front of the pack, you have to spend the money to get the latest, fastest tires, and you're going to want to invest in having your engine dyno-tuned periodically. It's conceivable, if you get serious about winning, that you'd even want a spare engine and gearbox to take along in case anything happened. If you were to do this, you could easily spend five or maybe even ten thousand dollars racing a Showroom sedan or a Formula Vee for a season. The same thing is true in any class of road racing; you have a spectrum of cost ranging from, say, five hundred to well over ten thousand dollars to campaign a car for a season.

In SCCA's production category, it can be fairly inexpensive to race a Sprite or one of the other small sports cars. Here, too, you could reduce your overall investment by also using it for your daily transportation. There was a time when this was fairly common and there have been instances where the owner drove his car to the race, won, and then drove it home again. This might happen even today in some areas but the chance of a driver winning a production category event on the east or west coast without a fully prepared, all-out car is remote.

Production category racing can also be extremely expensive. In those classes where factory-backed teams are active, I'm not sure that any individual entrant would think it could possibly be worth the money that is required. If a private individual wanted to campaign a car in one of these hotly contested classes with the same investment in personnel, development and equipment, it would have to cost him at least $50,000 for the season. And that would be for *one* car!

In the sports/racing category, there's an even greater range of expense. If you buy a ready-prepared but somewhat older D-sports/racing car you could probably get through a season as cheaply as in Formula Vee. But if you were to go all-out in DSR, you'd have $10,000 in your car before it ever turned a wheel and you could easily spend that much again campaigning it for a season. And if you were to go into the bigger classes, the price would go up proportionately. For one of the latest Can-Am cars, just the basic equipment would cost you close to $50,000 and you'd have to have a basic reserve of more than $100,000 if you planned to run the whole series.

In IMSA racing you can get started at relatively low cost, just as you can in SCCA, but IMSA does offer some kind of prize money in all their events, which gives you hope. But if you're going to get much of it, you're going to have to prepare your car up to the limit. And that costs the same kind of money.

It's possible that when you do become successful in almost any class of road racing, you will attract some form of financial assistance. Several of the production car manufacturers have performance bonus programs that offer as much as $500 for a class win in an SCCA National and you can often get a discount on parts through either a local dealer or the distributor. Nevertheless, there isn't enough money in any of these programs to keep anybody solvent who is racing his own car and paying his own way in road racing.

It's amazing how little some people know about sponsorship. I have had people come to me who have absolutely no experience in racing and request that either I sponsor them or give them the name of somebody else who would sponsor them *if* they got into racing. This simply shows a lack of knowledge about what is actually involved in racing. I remember an article in *Road & Track* by a young driver in the midwest who had been racing a Triumph Spitfire for three years, had set a couple lap records and was obviously a pretty fair driver in his class. He said that total extent of the sponsorship he'd received so far consisted of eight free spark plugs and the use of a friend's unheated garage.

So don't expect to find somebody to pay the bills before you've established yourself as not only a good driver but a successful driver. Getting a sponsor before you've done this, I think, is virtually impossible. And it's tough even then.

As for the kind of car you ought to race, that's up to your own preferences and pocketbook. Generally speaking, a lighter car will use up tires less quickly than a heavier one and the more powerful the car, the more it will cost you to run it. A Porsche 914/6, for instance, will go through a set of racing tires in one or two race weekends. And the best racing tires will cost you about $50 each, including mounting and balancing. But a Formula Vee, an HP or a DSR car could go through a whole season on the same set of tires.

As a general rule, I'd suggest that you start out with a production category car. What kind, as I said, is a matter for you to decide. But as there are some basic differences between front-engined and rear-engined cars, perhaps it would be helpful if I were to make some observations about some of the more popular ones so you can have a little better idea of the differences.

I'll put these production category cars in three basic groups—those with front engines and live rear axles, those with front engines and all-independent suspension, and those with the engines in the rear, or mid engine.

In the first category—front engine, live rear axle—there are the Sprite, MG, Triumph TR-4, Datsun roadster and so on. These are basic sports cars, fun to drive, reasonably inexpensive to maintain and are simple and straightforward enough that the backyard mechanic with basic hand tools can do just about everything that is needed to make them raceworthy. They are probably the simplest kinds of cars to race because there are only a few basic modifications you can make so far as suspension and chassis tuning is concerned and bolt-on equipment is readily available for these cars through the manufacturers' competition parts catalogs. That isn't to say they're the easiest cars to win with because the competition among them is just as tough as any other class. They are relatively easy to drive to

Cars with live rear axles are usually simpler to maintain.

their limits, are mostly predictable in their handling and you can learn a tremendous amount by spending a season or two in one of them. All of these cars are basically what are called understeering cars; that is, when the limit of the tires' adhesion is reached the front tires slide first and the front end of the car wants to go off the road. This is the kind of car that most of us grew up with since almost all American sedans are deliberately engineered with a large degree of early-warning understeer.

The examples in the second category—front engine but with independent rear suspension—are less numerous. Included are Triumph Spitfire and GT6, Triumph TR-4A, TR-250, TR-6, Datsun 240Z, later Corvette, E-type Jaguar, Cobra, Lotus Elan, etc. These are slightly more sophisticated machines than those in the first category, will generally corner a little faster (except on a dead smooth surface) and their handling, near the limit, is not quite so readily predictable by the less expert driver. Also, because of the added mechanical complication of the independent suspension, they are just that much more expensive to buy in the first place though not significantly more expensive to maintain once you've made the investment. A car with independent suspension is more difficult to prepare for competition because it is amenable to suspension tuning with such things as different anti-rollbars and springs. You can also tune the handling to suit your own driving preferences to some extent and make the handling more nearly neutral than with a live rear-axle car.

In the third category—rear engined cars—there are the various Porsche models, the Fiat 850, Lotus Europa, etc. These, for the beginner, I would say are the most complicated production category cars of all. Because the engine is in the rear, most of the weight is in the rear and when you lose adhesion, the rear end wants to come around, making it oversteer. That is, you get more reaction from the steering than you put into it. An oversteering car can be a tremendous amount of fun to drive, of course, because it is easier to hang the rear end out and control it with the throttle. But honestly, as sticky as modern racing tires are for production category cars these days, there's very little justification for hanging it out and it's almost always faster to drive through the corner with just as little sideways driving as possible. With a rear-engined car you have independent suspension with the possibility (and expense) of needing special parts for tuning the handling. Also, as a general rule, a rear-engined car will need new tires sooner than a front-engined car, especially on the rear, though this depends to a great extent on the driver's style.

There is another category that should be mentioned—those with front engines and front wheel drive. In this category are the Saab Sonett and, in small sedan racing, the various Mini Coopers. These are basically simple cars to prepare for racing because everything of major importance is at the same end of the car and there isn't much you can do (or that needs doing) at the rear. These are all true understeerers and the driving technique required for them is as specialized as that for a tail-heavy rear-engined car. With front wheel drive the more power you apply, the more it wants to go straight off the road in a turn or the power will pull around the turn, depending on your speed, and you have to develop a very smart throttle foot to learn just how much throttle to give it to get through fast but without going off the road. They are basically safe-handling cars, though, because all you have to do to decrease your turning radius is ease off on the throttle. And be ready to correct when you do that, of course; otherwise you'll go off the other side of the road. Or fall over.

The same generalities also apply to the various categories of sedans and GT cars in both SCCA and IMSA racing. Virtually all sports/racing cars these days are of mid-engine design. Except that most of them have more power than rear-engined production category cars (and also stick better in the turns because

SCCA "performance" classes often mix several types of cars.

there's almost no limit to the amount of rubber you can put on the road), the same basics apply to those.

Among Formula racing cars there are three basic varieties—Formula Vee, Formula Ford or Super Vee, and Formula SCCA. These true single-seater racing cars all have the engine behind the driver and all are great fun to drive. However, if safety is a factor in your decision, I wouldn't consider either Formula or sports/racing cars to start out in.

So we come back to the first question again—what kind of car should you race? All things considered, I'd suggest starting out in a production category sports or GT car. Showroom Stock would be the safest kind of car but I don't think it's quite serious enough to provide the kind of challenge you need. The various types of Formula cars rate further down the list as cars in which to start your career, and because of their complexities I'd rate sports/racing cars as the least desirable in which to start racing.

So make your start in a production category sports or GT car and I don't think you'll be sorry. These are good cars to learn in and there's plenty of time to work up into the more complicated types of machines.

Preparing the Car

OKAY, YOU'VE ABSORBED THE INFORMATION in the previous chapters, you've joined the club you're going to race with, you've read the right books, you have your subscription to *Autoweek,* you've gone to the races as a worker, pit crew member and spectator, you've worked out your budget and you've bought the car. Now what do you do to get ready?

If you've joined SCCA—and almost everyone who drives in road races in this country started with SCCA—you're going to hear a lot about safety. Maybe more than you really want to hear. But safety is one of the main concerns in club racing, not only because member-oriented organizations don't like to have members get injured, but also because it also affects the race insurance picture. And race insurance has become so expensive the last few years that there's a real danger that SCCA won't be able to hold races of the kind that you and I can afford to participate in.

So the first thing to worry about is making your car just as safe as possible. Both SCCA and IMSA require all cars to have rollover protection, a seat belt and shoulder harness and that the car be prepared in such a way as to instill confidence in the tech inspectors' hearts that the wheels aren't going to fall off or the fuel lines come loose and set the whole thing on fire. In addition, in some classes you are also required to have safety fuel tanks and other specialized equipment.

Before we get into the nutsy-boltsy stuff, let me again add a few words of caution about tech inspection crews as this is a major part of racing when you're getting started. When you go out for your first event, or even for driver training, a crew of these people will go over your car to make sure that it meets the safety regulations and that, in general, it conforms to the regulations governing legal preparation. As early as possible in your career you should get used to the fact that these tech inspectors are nit-picking, unimaginative, and scared to death of anything they haven't seen before. They aren't, the vast majority of them, qualified to make any decision related to inventive engineering. Anything they can find in your car to complain about, they will. If you didn't safety wire your shoulder harness mounting bolts because you were going to have to take it out again before the race, they'll find it and it will be like you were deliberately trying to commit suicide. They'll probably tell you over and over that all they're trying to do is keep you from killing yourself. And sometime, when you really do forget something important, all their nit-picking just may do that. So let them nit-pick. As if you had a choice.

So rule number one about car preparation is to have your car so well prepared when you get to tech inspection that they can poke and probe and peek all they like without finding anything to upset them. After they become familiar with you and your car and realize that you always run a very sanitary machine, they'll probably become your friends and you'll wonder what all the fuss was about when you first started.

One of the things tech inspectors worry about a lot is roll-bars. "Rollover protection," in racing, means a rollbar or a

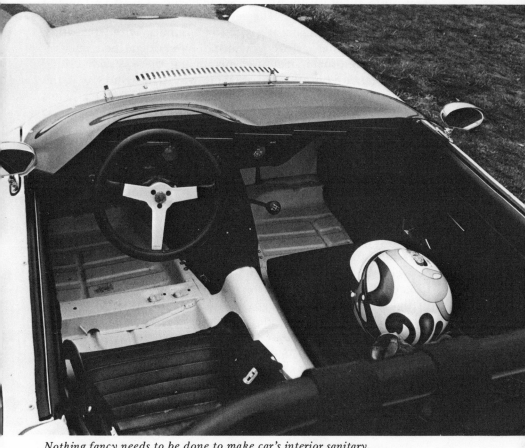

Nothing fancy needs to be done to make car's interior sanitary.

rollcage, not just a metal roof. There are companies that make rollbars for the more popular production category cars (see the classified section in *Autoweek*) and this is undoubtedly the simplest way to do it. Or you can make your own, or have one made. If you are going to do this, however, be sure that you're familiar with what's being done in other cars like yours and what is acceptable to your local tech inspectors. And be sure to conform to the rollbar specifications in the special appendix of the SCCA's GCR or the IMSA Code. You might design one that would be just as strong but if it doesn't look like something they've seen before, the tech crew will be skeptical.

The other major item of safety equipment in the car is the safety harness. The regulations require Air Force-quality belts at

33

least three inches wide for the lap belt and at least two inches wide over the shoulders. The regulations are pretty well spelled out for these but, again, it's wise to be familiar with what other drivers have done before you install yours. The belt anchors must go into a main structural member, if there is such a thing in your car, or be attached in some way that assures that the fastening bolts won't pull out. Some cars need reinforcing plates under the floorpan. Some require a whole sub-structure to be welded in to make the attaching points strong enough. My recommendation is to select mounting points that will hold you down rather than hold you back. Generally, the use of large washers for shoulder harness mounting points and something larger in the way of a metal plate for seat belt mountings will be acceptable. Everything must be double-nutted and I suggest the use of Loctite as well, just to be sure.

Also required, in addition to the lap and shoulder belts, is a fifth belt that fastens down in front of you and comes up between the legs to fasten into the main buckle. This is not only to keep you from submarining under the lap belt (which should fit tightly around your thighs) but also to keep the other belts from pulling up into the more vulnerable abdomen area in case of a collision where you are thrown forward.

These are the two main items of safety equipment that are required on all racing cars. Some cars also require stronger parts in order to stand up to the additional strain put on them in competition, such as clutch scatter shields, special hubs or stronger wheels, and again these are things you can find out by becoming familiar with the regulations before you start racing.

Because dependability is of utmost importance during the learning phase of your career, I'm going to suggest that instead of doing those things that will give your car more power, you concentrate on the things that will make it dependable. Tune your stock engine so that it will run just as well as the manufacturer intended it to run but don't start out by buying trick cams and reworking the head. What you want is a car that will run and run and run and let you learn to drive in competition without having to worry too much about extracting the last ounce of power. If you do that, you'll spend too much of your time keeping the car running and not enough learning to drive.

In getting your car ready, make sure that it is easy to drive. The regulations allow you to replace the driver's seat with any type of special driving seat but for most drivers, the stock seat will do in the beginning. Make sure that your seating position is the right one for you so you can comfortably reach the steering

When learning, you don't need the most expensive type of wheels.

35

wheel, shift lever, pedals and other controls. Be sure that you don't have anything that interferes with your normal movements when you're driving, like a doorknob or window winder you can hit your arm or hand on. Or a floormat that can catch your foot. You're permitted to remove the floormats and this will avoid that hazard. If the aesthetics bother you, spray the floor with Zolatone or flat black paint to make it look professional.

Be sure that everything is working properly. The brakes should be fresh, or near fresh, and with plenty of lining or pad material to see you through the event. The brakes should also be properly adjusted so that you can make a hands-off stop from, say, 60 mph without the car pulling to the left or right. The clutch should be in proper adjustment and above all, not slipping under full acceleration. Your gearbox should be trouble-free and while not absolutely essential, it's helpful if all the synchromeshes are working properly.

Under the hood the valves, points and plugs should be set at the manufacturers' recommended clearances. All the fuel line connections should be tight with clamps added per the rules. The fuel pump has to be capable of delivering enough fuel to keep the car in continuous operation at full throttle. And water hoses should be in new or as-new condition.

It's important that the float bowls in your carburetors be adjusted to the proper level so they don't starve out and cause the engine to falter in the turns. This is not as easy as it sounds. There are turns on every circuit where the lateral acceleration (side thrust) is such that the float level becomes critical and you can experience a large stumble if it isn't right. There's nothing that will destroy your concentration like being all set up for a turn, preparing for just the right moment to turn on the power and then have the car cough and stumble just when you need to make a smooth transition from power off to power on.

Before you go out to drive in competition for the first time, you'll probably think about wheels and tires. Tires, especially, are extremely important in road racing today. But unless you're ready to make an all-out investment in the lightest alloy wheels and the stickiest racing tires, you'll be better off to use something a little heavier in the way of wheels (wider steel wheels, for instance, instead of mags) and a tire that has a little harder rubber compound as it will last a lot longer than the best racing tire. The most important thing at this stage is learning, not spending as much money as possible. In any case, no matter what you decide about tires, be sure that you have enough rubber when you go out so you don't have to worry about how much tread you have left. As for tire pressures, you probably won't have access to a skid pad so the best thing you can do is find out what pressures other cars of about the same weight as your car and equipped with the same kind of tires are using. In general, racing tires require higher pressures than street tires and you have to work out the combination that suits your car best. Remember to take into consideration that pressures will build as your tires heat up on the race track.

When you get ready to go to the circuit, make sure everything is done before you start. Don't plan on finishing the car preparation after you arrive. Don't forget car numbers and class designation; put them on the car before you get to the track. Don't forget the basic tools you'll need. Be sure that your windows are clean inside and out. Be sure that all the loose objects in the cockpit are removed so you won't find them rolling around under your feet just when you don't need them.

Remember, if you're going out to learn about driving, it is of utmost importance that the car be dependable.

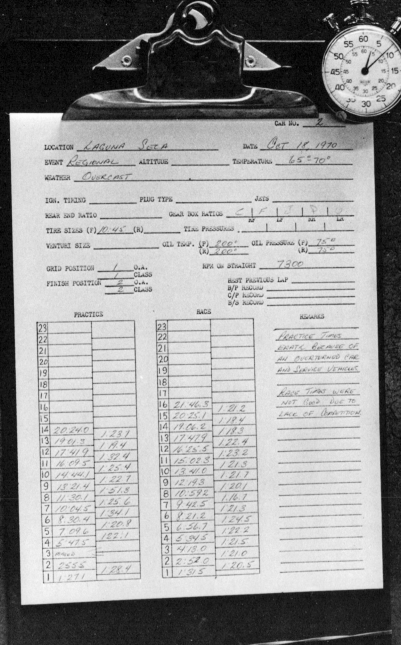

CAR NO. 2

LOCATION _Laguna Seca_   DATE _Oct 18, 1970_
EVENT _Regional_   ALTITUDE _____   TEMPERATURE _65°-70°_
WEATHER _Overcast_

IGN. TIMING _____   PLUG TYPE _____   JETS _____
REAR END RATIO _____   GEAR BOX RATIOS C F J P O
TIRE SIZES (F) _10.45_ (R) _____   TIRE PRESSURES ___ RF | LF | RR | LR
VENTURI SIZES _____   OIL TEMP. (F) _200°_ OIL PRESSURE (F) _75°_
                            (R) _200°_   (R) _75°_

GRID POSITION _1_ O.A.   RPM ON STRAIGHT _7300_
              _1_ CLASS
FINISH POSITION _2_ O.A.   BEST PREVIOUS LAP _____
                _2_ CLASS   B/P RECORD _____
                               C/P RECORD _____
                               B/S RECORD _____

PRACTICE			RACE			REMARKS
23			23			
22			22			Practice times
21			21			erratic because of
20			20			an overturned car
19			19			and service vehicles
18			18			
17			17			Race times were
16			16	21:46.3	1:21.2	not good due to
15			15	20:25.1	1:18.4	lack of competition
14	20:24.0	1:23.7	14	19:06.2	1:18.3	
13	19:01.3	1:19.4	13	17:47.9	1:22.4	
12	17:41.9	1:32.4	12	16:25.5	1:23.2	
11	16:09.5	1:25.4	11	15:02.3	1:21.3	
10	14:44.1	1:22.7	10	13:41.0	1:21.7	
9	13:21.4	1:51.8	9	12:19.3	1:20.1	
8	11:30.1	1:25.6	8	10:59.2	1:16.7	
7	10:04.5	1:34.1	7	9:42.5	1:21.3	
6	8:30.4	1:20.8	6	8:21.2	1:24.5	
5	7:09.6	1:22.1	5	6:56.7	1:22.2	
4	5:47.5		4	5:34.5	1:21.5	
3	missed		3	4:13.0	1:21.0	
2	2:55.5	1:28.4	2	2:52.0	1:20.5	
1	1:27.1		1	1:31.5		

The Crew

AN ESSENTIAL PART of any driver's race car effort is his pit crew. There will come a time and probably very soon in your racing career when you'll need help from someone in the pits. You'll need something done and won't be able to do it yourself because you happen to be driving the car or there's too much for one person to do. At a time like this you'll want the best help possible. This help won't just happen—you'll have to plan for it. Even the first day you go to driver's training, it is extremely important to have someone along who shares your enthusiasm for what you're doing. In road racing, very often the driver's wife fulfills the basic function as the crew and does very well at it. I've seen contestants at the National championships where the entire crew consisted of a driver and wife.

When you're not actually on the track, as well as during practice or a race, you need a pit crew because, as a driver, you'll have so many things to do and think about that you'll miss something if your crew doesn't see that it is done. You always will. It's inevitable. Delegate all the responsibility you can when you're at the track. This enables you to concentrate on those things that are most important to you. Like driving.

In no particular order of importance, here are some of the things you could make your crew responsible for:

Make sure you have enough food and drink to make your stay at the track as comfortable as possible. There may be a concession stand open when you need it or there may not. And in any case you can generally do better from a victuals point of view by bringing your own than eating the concessionaire's.

When assigning work to be done on the car be careful to specify as clearly as possible just what you want done and how you want it done. Misunderstandings with pit crews have cost a lot of races.

Be sure that somebody has the responsibility for knowing the schedule of events. Find out when your class is scheduled for practice and be sure the essential members of your crew know what time you will need to have them there. Crew members that can't make an early morning practice session, you don't need.

It's important that your lap times be kept. Without lap times, you don't really know how you're doing.

When you start racing, decide from the very first time you go out that you're going to have complete records on your car and your performance. A crew member can do this for you, if you have one you can depend on. Record everything you do, every change you make in the car, what your tire pressures were when you went out and came in from the course, what the shock absorber settings were, what plugs you were using and whatever else there is on the car that might need changing. Record the oil temperature, the water temperature, how many revs you used and the maximum revs you were pulling down the longest straight. Be sure to record your gear ratios. And keep lap times in your files for next year. All these things are invaluable, especially when you go back to the same course again and you don't want to have to start over from the beginning as if you'd never been there before. Several racing accessory companies offer spe-

cial forms for recording all the above information and a lot more. You'll find advertisements for these things in *Autoweek*. Or you could devise your own and have them Xeroxed.

And know your competition. Once you're past driver training, you'll be picking out the other drivers you're going to be racing with. So have your crew get lap times on those drivers as well. And that too goes into your notebook so the next time you race at that course you'll know whether you're gaining or losing on your competition.

You'll probably want to develop a system for pit signals; both those your crew sends you and those you use to communicate with them. There are almost as many variations in pit signals as there are cars. I started out with a chalk board and in the early days my crew sent me enough information during a race to fill a book. Later we went on to the fancier type metal board with magnetic numbers and the information was pretty much restricted to where I stood, my lap times, who was ahead of me (and how far) and who was behind (and how far). When I was driving for Richie Ginther, a real pro, he used to come out to the pit wall and give me very simple hand signals. Up, okay. Ahead, step on it. Behind, slow down. Plus some simple variations. It really worked. We also knew before going out on

the course just about what lap times we'd be turning from our records and from comparisons made with other classes, and we discussed what his hand signals would mean on this course.

Giving pit signals is also good for your crew. It gives them something to do besides worry. If they are giving you a signal every lap, they really feel like they're helping you in the race. And I don't mean to belittle their contribution because there are times when pit signals are extremely important. Admittedly, however, for most SCCA club races, which rarely last more than a half hour, you're usually going just as fast as you can and most of the information you get from your crew is superfluous.

The basic information you want to receive from your crew is how you're doing, where you stand in the race, or in your class, and how much longer the race has to go and maybe your lap times. Sometimes, usually from loss of concentration, you slow down without knowing it and it's good to be told about it. Sometimes, if you're gaining on the driver ahead, it's helpful to know who it is and how far ahead he is. Or if somebody is gaining on you, how quickly he's coming up.

In your position as the driver, you're limited in the amount of information you can transmit to your crew. If your clutch is slipping, there's little they can do about it at that stage and it's of little value to them at that moment. If you're coming in for fuel the next time around, you can work out something for that. Or if you have a tire going soft, you can give them a pre-determined signal to alert them to have the jack ready. But if you're running hot, the oil pressure is sinking, your brakes are gone and you're only trying to hold on and finish, you can tell them about it when the race is over.

And when you get back to the pits and have cooled off, put it all down in your notebook.

And don't forget to give credit to your crew for their efforts. When you get your chance to take a victory lap make sure you take your crew with you—all of them if possible. They deserve a share of the glory. Especially if your pit crew is your wife.

And the Driver

JUST AS THE CAR and the crew must be prepared so must the driver prepare himself. As well as being worried about the safety equipment that is required on the car itself, the clubs also worry a lot about the equipment that is worn by the driver. And this is good as it tends to minimize the dangers when the irresistible meets the unavoidable or when enthusiasm overcomes driving skill, experience, or good sense.

Before you arrive at the course for your first race, you'll have to have a helmet, goggles or face shield (unless you're driving a closed car), a driving suit, gloves, socks and shoes.

The regulations spell all this out and tell you what's approved with each organization but I'm going to offer some suggestions.

EQUIPMENT

Helmet. Get yourself a helmet that fits properly, get it in plenty of time and don't leave it till the last minute. The best helmet you can buy is the helmet your head should have. I prefer Bell helmets. I've never put one to the ultimate test but I know a good many drivers who have and if anything happens to you—and it can—I think you're better off in a Bell.

If you are driving a car with an open cockpit, be sure to get the Bell Star, which is the full-coverage type. It's also a good idea to wear one in a closed car. It's a little embarrassing and strange at first and there have been some well known drivers who regarded it as sissy to wear such a helmet. These are some of the USAC old guard, but even they are coming around. Let me tell you a little story. Denis Hulme had an incident during practice at Indianapolis in 1970 that you may have heard about. A fuel filler cap popped open, letting fuel run into the cockpit and it caught fire. His hands were very badly burned and as a result he was out of action for several weeks. He was wearing a Bell Star helmet and although the front of it was badly charred, he didn't receive any facial burns at all. The Bell Star offers a little bit of added insurance and is well worth the extra cost.

Driving suits. I recommend the full-length, one-piece suit or a two-piece suit where the top tucks well into the pants. Let me tell you another story. Dr. Lou Sell, who won the Formula A championship that year, crashed in a USAC race at Riverside in the latter part of 1968. His car caught fire while he was upside down and it was only because he was wearing one of the fire-resistant driver suits that he lived at all. But he was wearing a two-piece suit where the top did not tuck into the pants. His most serious burns were on his stomach and chest where the two parts of the suit pulled apart.

The most expensive injuries to repair on the human body are burns—as well as being the most painful, I should think. First it was flame-resistant cotton, then it was Nomex, then it was Pro-tex, then it was something newer and better and next year it will probably be something still better. SCCA's requirements for flame-resistant driver's suits have saved so many drivers that we all take them for granted by this time. It wasn't always this way. Remember the pictures of Juan Manuel Fangio when he was racing? He wore short-sleeved polo shirts to race in. And many drivers raced in T-shirts. Like Ken Miles. He believed that he was safest when he was most comfortable and was really indignant when he first had to wear a long-sleeved outfit. Later he gave it more thought and became an advocate of the best personal safety equipment. And fortunately, since the recent advances in fireproof and fire-resistant synthetic fabrics, many of the leading drivers—like Jackie Stewart, for instance—have become outspoken advocates of better racing safety equipment and this has done wonders for making it acceptable.

Shoes. You should have comfortable shoes that are light in weight and easy to drive in. They are required to be made of leather, without perforations, and there are fire-resistant socks that you are also required to wear. Your shoes should fit snugly and the soles should not stick out lest they momentarily get caught under the edge of the pedal when you're trying to get your foot off the gas and onto the brake. Many a driver has had this happen and it can really mess you up.

Gloves. SCCA allows you to wear either leather gloves or ones made of flame-resistant material but you should not wear ones made completely of leather. Leather, when exposed to fire, tends to shrink and shrink badly. When Denis Hulme's hands were so badly burned in the Indy accident, it was largely because his gloves shrunk so much and so quickly that he could not get them off. Incidentally, where his body was covered with his driving suit and his head covered by the full-coverage helmet, he was not burned at all. His hands were burned, and his feet, too, where the fuel got in through the vent holes in the leather shoes.

If you're driving an open car and don't choose the Bell Star helmet, be sure to get goggles that fit and are comfortable for you. I've gone through the whole thing with goggles. First I got the keen-looking type with the smoked glass and split lenses. The kind Phil Hill used to wear. I thought I looked great, like a real race driver, and I spent a lot of money on them. But pretty soon the glass got scratched and I couldn't see out of them very well. So I bought some more that weren't quite as expensive and the same thing happened. After a while I was buying Air Force-surplus goggles for about $2 a pair which looked terrible and worked great. I recommend them highly. When the lens gets scratched, you put in a new one for 50 cents. If you get too much sun, you put a piece of tape across them to give you shade. Motorcycle shops sell the same type for a little more money and those with felt padding are more comfortable.

If you wear glasses, or even if you don't, you may prefer a face shield. Certainly you should have one in your equipment

47

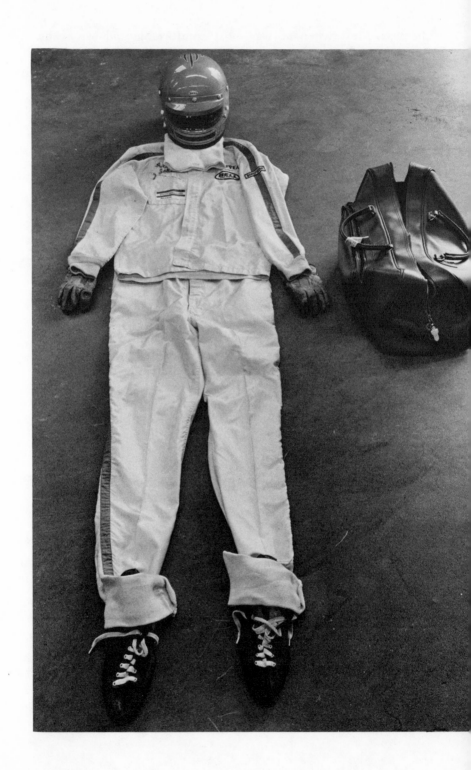

You need the equipment (left) and someplace to keep it (above).

bag for use when it rains since they don't fog up like goggles when it's wet. The Paulsen Bubble Shield is probably the most satisfactory of the face shield types and also the safest since it is of thin, pliable material that is less likely to cut you if you bounce your face off the dashboard or the ground.

When you're fully equipped with all your personal safety gear, put it in a big flight bag so it will always be all together. Use a plenty big one as you'll accumulate extra gear as you go along and maybe want room to carry a spare set of fireproof underwear when the weather is hot and you don't look forward on Sunday to climbing into those that were somewhat gamey after Saturday's race.

When you first get dressed up in your outfit, you may feel a little self-conscious about it. That's normal. Most of us do. But when you're fully equipped with all the best gear, it also makes you feel like a race driver. After a while you won't feel like racing without the very best equipment available.

ATTITUDE

Your mental attitude is extremely important when you begin working to become a competition driver. You'll probably have the feeling that you're already a pretty competent driver before you start. If you didn't, you wouldn't be considering going racing in the first place. But it's important to keep an open mind about racing. Say to yourself, "There may be something I can learn." And you'll be very unusual indeed if there isn't something you *can* learn about competition driving. The better drivers are almost always those who are ready to learn something new about driving.

When you go into driver training, an instructor will probably be assigned to you. In SCCA these instructors are all volunteers and while they don't all have the same level of competence as teachers, they are all experienced drivers and there should be something you can learn from any one of them.

It's also important to ask questions. And don't be afraid to ask a question because you think it might be dumb. Those are often the most important questions of all and sometimes are the very questions that everybody in the group is wondering about. Also challenge the answers you get from your instructor if they don't sound right to you. Don't be a wise guy but make him explain it so you can understand the point he's trying to make. Also test the things you're told, see if they work for you even if you don't think they make a lot of sense at first. Most of all, keep your mind receptive to different ideas. This is tremendously important all the way through your driving career if you're ever going to progress beyond being merely competent.

One of the things that will be required of you in competition driving is a level of concentration you've probably never experienced before. This is absolutely essential. It's required turn after turn and lap after lap. The more effectively you concentrate on your driving, the better—and faster—you'll go. This doesn't mean you're going to be tense. You shouldn't be. You should be relaxed. But you want to concentrate on everything you do. If you're going into a turn, concentrate on doing it exactly right. At one place on the course where you have time to do it, glance at the instruments. The middle of the straight will probably be the best spot to do this. If you're concentrating, they'll tell you what you want to know. When you get to the next turn, concentrate on braking at exactly the right point, planning ahead to the shift you're going to make and the exact line you want to be on when you leave the turn. Don't let your mind wander. If you do, you'll slow down. It's inevitable. I've talked to a lot of drivers about this. I remember what Dan Gurney said after he had come in 3rd or 4th in the Italian Grand Prix a few years ago. When I asked why, since he was over a lap ahead of the next driver, he didn't ease off, Dan said he didn't dare. Once you break your concentration, deliberately slowing down, you break your rhythm and you can't get it back. I've seen it happen time after time. If you want to save the car, use fewer revs. Shift at 6500 instead of 7000. But keep your concentration and go just as fast as you can. Concentration is the key. And it pays off, believe me.

Another short story on concentration. I was in my very first real race back in 1960. I was driving my Porsche Speedster in 2nd position in class and turning fairly consistent lap times. I began watching the car behind me in my rear view mirror and the more I watched the worse my lap times were because I was being distracted. The car caught me and had no trouble passing, but as soon as he'd passed, my lap time picked back up and I was able to stay right with him. I later learned to turn down the rear view mirror to avoid being distracted and eventually was able to maintain concentration without turning it down—even with someone right on my rear bumper.

Open-mindedness and concentration—two keys to driver preparation.

Basic Competition Driving Techniques

THE BASIC TECHNIQUES employed in competition driving are, in many ways, simply exaggerations of what you do in your ordinary, everyday driving. You accelerate, you shift gears, you brake and you turn. It's the same in racing except that there are a few additional wrinkles and refinements.

First of all, your position behind the wheel. You should sit snugly but comfortably, directly behind the wheel, square with the pedals and the shift lever at a distance where you can make the farthest-away shift without having to lean forward. You should also be able to see the essential instruments without

53

Reach should be "comfortable;" not too close, not too far.

having to move your head. If one instrument is in the wrong place, move it.

You drive with both hands on the steering wheel, the left one usually between the nine and ten o'clock positions, the right between two and three. The steering wheel should be a comfortable distance away from you, neither too close nor too far. You should be close enough that you can make a full cross-arm on the rim, almost a full half-turn of the wheel, without having to lean forward to reach the top of the wheel or having your elbows touch your body. There are other schools of thought, of course. I think it was Giuseppe Farina who popularized the straight-arm driving style and while it admittedly looks classic, it has been responsible for more aching shoulders and backs than it's really worth in terms of driving efficiency. When your arms are extended straight out, the muscles behind your shoulders are the ones that are doing the work and they aren't accustomed to that until they've been specially developed for it. It's a lot more natural to let the elbows bend a little. And a lot less tiring. In this position it's mostly the arm muscles that do the work in a natural pull-and-push motion they're used to.

Being too close to the steering wheel is equally bad, though for a different reason. If you're too close, you can't make a full half-turn of the steering wheel without being awkward.

The location of the other controls is equally important. Your pedals should be located at the right distance and nothing should interfere with the movement of your legs when you operate them. Ideally, the pedals should be far enough away that your legs still have a little bend in the knee when they are at the bottom of their travel. You have more leverage this way, it's faster to move your foot when the leg is almost at full length and it is more comfortable than sitting with a lot of bend in your knees. You should have a place to rest your heel when your foot is on the accelerator: either the bend in the floorboard, which comes at the right place in many cars, or a special heel rest that puts the accelerator pedal under the ball of your foot. This is important because your heel can then act as the pivot point for your foot and you can control your pressure on the accelerator much more delicately.

There's nothing in the rules that keeps you from moving (or even replacing) the pedals so they will be in the right position for you. I like the throttle and brake pedals close together and adjusted so they're at just about the same level when the brake

You should be able to turn wheel 180 degrees without strain.

is full on. This makes it easier to "heel-and-toe." The pedals should also be covered with a non-slip material so your foot has a sure grip. Rubber pads are all right when they are dry but water or oil will make them slippery and carborundum-faced tape is better as its grip is certain under all conditions.

BE SMOOTH

The car should be driven just as smoothly as possible at all times. This is very important, especially when you're learning. Smoothness will become even more important later when you're trying to get the last little bit off your lap time for qualifying or to outrun a competitor. Get into the habit of working on this in your everyday driving. Don't stab the accelerator; squeeze it on and let it off smoothly. Don't slam on the brakes; apply them deliberately, increasing the pressure to get maximum braking without skidding. Don't yank on the steering wheel; move it thoughtfully, feeling what is going on. The best drivers are the smoothest drivers; this has been proven time after time and in all kinds of racing.

The primary reason for being smooth is to keep the car as well balanced as possible at all times. By "balance," I mean having the weight equally distributed on all four wheels. Jerk the steering wheel and the car leans over on the suspension, lifting the weight on the springs and unloading the inside wheels. Then it has to come back down again, settling the weight on all four tires before the car is balanced again. During the time that the suspension is in its transient condition, the geometry is screwed up and not operating at maximum efficiency. Your steering is less effective, the tires have less adhesion and your brakes can't work as well. No matter how smoothly you drive you can't avoid these transients altogether but if you are driving smoothly, they will be much less abrupt and when you make a turn your car will balance up that much more quickly. This enables you to apply power that much sooner coming off a turn and cut that part of a second off your lap time.

Carroll Shelby, who was the first person I ever heard talk about the importance of "balance" in this way, says that Stirling Moss was quicker at getting a racing car balanced than any driver he had ever seen. Shelby said that he could always outbrake Moss (given equal cars) but Moss was always that little bit quicker at getting his car balanced and this let him get onto the throttle just that little bit quicker than anybody else.

Smoothness is also important in braking. If you stand on the pedal, the car dives, the nose going down, lightening the rear end and reducing the traction. If you apply the brakes smoothly, the car has more of a tendency to squat and this keeps all four tires firmly planted, thus increasing the effectiveness of your brakes.

Also apply the throttle smoothly. You don't cram it to the floorboard when you want to accelerate, you feed it on just fast enough to give the engine all the fuel it can efficiently use at that instant. And in a turn where you can't apply full throttle all at once, you squeeze it on, almost feeling with your toes exactly how much the car will take and still hold the smooth line you want to follow out of the turn.

You really can improve your smoothness in driving with constant practice and I believe it is super important, but educating your feet and hands isn't as easy as it sounds. Begin working right now on driving as smoothly as possible all the time and you'll find that adding speed—when you're on a race track—will come more easily.

Make every shift smoothly and deliberately. This doesn't mean slowly, obviously. But with precision and care. I remember seeing a movie showing Fangio driving a racing car. I was amazed at the gentleness with which he handled the shift lever. Just gentle little flicks. If the shift knob had been an egg, he wouldn't have broken it. Lots of drivers tend to take out their frustrations on the shift lever, slamming it from one slot to another. Don't fall into that habit. It's better to swear a lot.

The smoothness that you develop is extremely important on all racing circuits. In fast bends, especially, smoothness is important because if you nail the throttle—or back off suddenly—you can get yourself in serious trouble.

If you drive smoothly, concentrating on all these basic driving techniques, you will find that you become much more sensitive to everything the car is doing. You begin to develop a feel for balance in a car, your throttle foot develops a cunning all its own and when your car does something that surprises you either because you did something clumsy or because you let your concentration lapse, you'll be embarrassed because of it. Or you should be. But most important, you'll feel it because you've trained yourself to be aware.

DOUBLE CLUTCHING

Double clutching (or, as the British say, double de-clutching) is a basic technique you'll want to master for competition driving. Most drivers already know how to double clutch but just so

57

Pedals should be at right distance, knees slightly bent.

we don't overlook anything, let me describe how it's done and explain why it's done.

You double clutch when you go from a higher to a lower gear. From third to second, say. There are three steps: (1) Push in on the clutch pedal, move the shift lever to neutral and release the clutch; (2) Press the accelerator, bringing the revs up; and (3) Depress the clutch pedal, shift into the lower gear and release the clutch. It's faster than it sounds. With practice it becomes very fast. In-shift-out, gas, in-shift-out, gas.

This is done to lessen the strain on the gearbox and drive train. By bringing the revs up in step 2, the shift lever will slide into the lower gear not only more easily but more quickly as well. With modern transmissions equipped with the better synchronizers, it isn't absolutely necessary to double clutch, of course, but it's a lot easier on everything if you do. Try it for yourself both ways and you'll see what I mean. Get up to about 4000 revs in third gear and dump it into second without double clutching and you'll feel the jerk and probably get a little chirp from the tires as well, telling you the shock loadings on the whole drive train. Doing it at the same speed but double clutching, you'll find that it happens more smoothly.

This is another basic driving technique that you can practice in your everyday driving. You'll be surprised how fast you can become at it and how it will become almost second nature.

DOWN SHIFTING

There isn't much I need to tell you about down shifting, really. The important thing is to double clutch to make it all happen more quickly and to lessen the strain on the drive train. But you also have to slow down enough in one gear so that you don't overrev the engine when you shift down. If you're tearing along at, say, 120 mph with the tach needle on the redline at 6000 rpm, you don't just dump it into the next lower gear. If you do that, the revs will pop up to something like 8000 and in most cars that would be enough to bend the valves and possibly blow the whole thing up. So you brake down to a speed that won't cause the revs to go past the redline when you complete your downshift. Using our example above, you'd have to brake

It's called heel-and-toe but this is how it's done on a Porsche.

down to about 90 mph before completing your downshift so the engine wouldn't be turning more than 6000 rpm after the clutch was released. So get to know your speeds in each gear. Work them out mathematically, if you need to, and put a mark on the tachometer face to show you how much you have to slow down before it's safe to shift down to each gear. Pretty soon it will become second nature to you and you will be shifting up and down automatically and probably using engine noise as much as the tach for a guide.

There will be times, after you've mastered the basic techniques of competition driving, when you will skip gears in downshifting, going directly from fifth to second, for instance. But we'll talk about that later; it's much easier on the car to go through each gear and that's what you should do through your learning period.

HEEL-AND-TOE

You hear a lot about "heel-and-toe" in competition driving but it really isn't an accurate description of what is done. Or at least it isn't the way I do it. I use the left side of my right foot on the brake, the right side on the throttle and I don't use my heel for anything except a pivot point. In earlier times, some racing cars had the throttle located below the brake or between the brake and clutch pedals and you actually used your heel on the throttle and your toe on the brake. But if you're much younger than Carroll Shelby, you won't ever have driven a car that was set up that way.

The reason you "heel-and-toe" is so you can brake and double clutch at the same time. For example, you are coming down the straightaway in fourth gear, you want to slow down as quickly as possible, and you don't want to take your foot off the brake to double clutch. So you apply the brake with the left side of your foot, roll your foot over onto the throttle (still braking) to bring the revs up as you double-clutch and maybe even continue to brake after completing the downshift. It's the next best thing to having three feet.

On some cars, you have to move the throttle pedal a little to the left so you can do this conveniently. It is also sometimes necessary to adjust the throttle pedal so it is at about the same height from the floorboard as the brake pedal under heavy braking. Some drivers relocate the throttle pedal so it is down closer to the heel and then use the toe on the brake pedal. But if you do this you don't have a steady pivot point for your foot and I think it is more difficult to modulate the pressure you put on

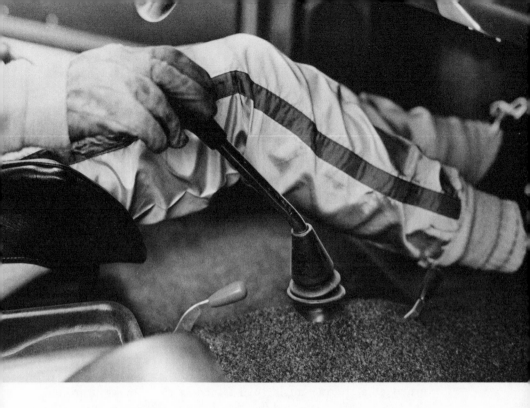

the throttle and brake. Maybe you'll want to try it both ways and see which works best for you. Be sure to check to make sure you're still getting full throttle after making any adjustments.

OVERSTEER & UNDERSTEER

Neutral steer, oversteer and understeer are ways of describing the way a car behaves while sliding or drifting in a turn. By the way, "sliding" is when the car has lost traction and is slowing down. "Drifting" is when the car has lost traction but is gaining speed. Ideally you'd slide into a turn and drift out, but if you were too fast or put too much power on too early you could end up sliding coming out of a turn. That's bad. With neutral steering, all four tires develop about the same slip angle and the rear wheels exactly follow the front ones. An oversteering condition is one where the rear tires have a greater slip angle than the fronts, the arc of the turn is made tighter and the rear end tends to move out. A car is understeering when the front tires have a greater slip angle than the rear and the arc of the turn is made greater. Let me try to say it another way. With neutral steer, the car follows around the turn as if on rails. With oversteer, the back end wants to come around and the nose of the car is pointed at the inside of the turn. With understeer, the front end wants to go straight and the nose is pointed toward the outside of the turn.

At normal touring speeds, most cars have neutral steering. As you drive faster, however, certain characteristics cause it to either oversteer or understeer. A rear-engined car, because of the weight of the engine, will probably be an oversteering car. And a front-engined car, for the same reason, will usually understeer. Suspension characteristics also have an effect on understeer and oversteer and some rear-engine cars achieve pretty nearly neutral steering through the use of wider tires (and hence more traction) at the rear.

In competition driving, however, you sometimes need to force the car into steering attitudes that are not in line with their basic characteristics. You can make what is basically an oversteering car understeer and vice versa. This is something you have to learn how to do, of course, and it takes practice. As you enter the turn, steer into the turn so that your wheels are turned at a sharper angle than is necessary to make it around the turn on its true radius. At the same time, squeeze the throttle, which makes the car want to widen the radius, adding enough throttle so that the rear end wants to push the front. You'll feel the front end want to go toward the outside of the turn and here you establish a delicate balance to get just the right amount of throttle and the right amount of steering to go through the rest of the turn just as quickly and as smoothly as possible.

If you jerk the steering wheel as you go into the turn, the car will slide sideways and when you do this, your tires scrub and you lose forward speed. If you're going too fast later in the turn, you'll have to let off the throttle to keep from going off the road and this will also cost you time. So do it smoothly, gradually working up to the speed where it all happens just right and you can actually feel what is happening with the car.

There are few modern sports cars that oversteer normally—unlike the Porsches of a few years back—but you can also force a car to oversteer when that happens to be the fastest way around a particular bend. These are usually very, very tight bends of the sort more likely to be found on a slalom course than a racing circuit and here what you want to do is throw the rear end out and have enough power turned on to keep it out until the car is pointing in the direction you want it to go. In

European rallying these are called "handbrake turns" because the rallyists will grab the handbrake, lock up the rear wheels with it, forcing the back end to slide around where they want it. Some cars used in trials and other competition events with very tight turns have what is called a "fiddle brake" which, when pulled up, locks one rear wheel and when pushed down, locks the other. But as I said, not many racing circuits have turns that are sharp enough to make these things necessary. To force a car into an oversteering condition, back off the throttle while entering the turn. This will usually tend to let the rear end come out. By working up your speed you can learn to keep it out.

PRACTICE ALL THE TIME

Most of these basic driving techniques we've been discussing are ones that you can practice and perfect in your everyday driving. You don't have to be on a race track. I practice all the time. No matter where I'm driving or what I'm driving. I'm working at it all the time. This is something I picked up from Dan Gurney. This doesn't mean that I'm exceeding the speed limit but it does mean that I'm paying attention to my driving, concentrating on what I'm doing, being critical of what I do and being alert to everything that is going on around me. I concentrate on driving smoothly, keeping my car exactly where I want it at all times, picking out the exact spot where I want to have my wheels when I turn a corner, stopping smoothly with the front bumper exactly six inches from the crosswalk at a signal and modulating my braking effort as I stop so that I can't even feel the exact moment when the car comes to a complete halt.

Nobody is ever so good that they don't need constant practice at driving. So practice all the time. You can't get too much.

A side benefit to learning to drive smoothly is that your wife or girl friend won't scream until a higher speed is reached.

Some of these cars are obviously not on the right line for turn.

Some Finer Points

WHEN A DRIVER GOES out onto a racing circuit to put together a fast lap, there are any number of ways he can go about it. He can, for example, regard each corner separately, driving through each one as fast as he can, hauling down the straightaways as rapidly as his car will take him and going as deeply into each corner as his brakes will allow. That sounds like it ought to work, doesn't it? Some drivers make the mistake of thinking that's all there is to it.

There's more to it than that. A lot more, as a matter of fact. All turns *aren't* of equal importance and in getting the fastest possible lap time it's as necessary to know where to brake early and go slow as it is to brake late and go fast. Different types of turns have varying degrees of importance. Knowing where to brake and how much to brake is essential. And taking advantage of the changes in elevation on both turns and straights is also necessary in making the fastest lap time.

In analyzing any road circuit, I consider that there are three types of turns and *only* three types of turns. In order of importance, let's call them Type I turns, Type II turns and Type III turns. A Type I turn, which is most important in terms of lap speed, is a turn that leads onto a straightaway. A Type II turn, which is the next most important, is one that comes at the end of a straightaway. And a Type III turn, the least important, is a turn that comes between turns.

This way of thinking applies to all road racing circuits and can also be applied to all slalom, gymkhana, autocross, time trial and hillclimb courses as well. If a driver will concentrate on Type I turns first, those that lead onto straightaways, and practice them until he does them perfectly, I guarantee he'll lower his lap times. Type II turns, although also as important, are less significant in terms of lap speed. And the Type III turns between turns are of almost no importance at all so far as lap speeds are concerned.

TYPE I TURN

In a Type I turn, one which leads onto a straightaway, the object is to get onto the straight going as fast as possible. This permits working up to maximum speed more quickly and lets the car go just as fast as possible for as long as possible. This is where races are won. On the straightaways. Not in the turns. And don't let anybody try to tell you otherwise.

The basic pattern for driving a Type I turn is this: Enter the turn on the outside of the road, shift down, brake and have all your braking done before you have much more than started to steer from the outside toward the inside of the turn. Then get a shade of throttle on as early as possible, keep moving closer to the inside, coming the closest about two-thirds of the way through the turn. Add more throttle to accelerate the rest of the way out of the turn in one smooth, continuous line. It is more important to maintain a correct line through a Type I turn than any other.

So you set up early, get the car balanced early, begin acceleration early and come out going like gangbusters.

In a Type I turn, a late apex is used. The apex of a turn is that point where you stop going into a turn and start coming out, the spot where you're closest to the inside edge of the road.

In most Type I turns, the apex will be about two-thirds of the way around the radius of the turn. When the car reaches the apex in a Type I turn the throttle should be pretty nearly full on so the acceleration will gradually widen the arc until the car uses up the entire width of the road and approaches the outside edge of the straightaway as the car exits the turn.

The balance of the car is critical in a Type I turn. A touch of very light throttle is necessary just as early as possible in order to set the suspension and get the tires firmly planted on the road, then the throttle is squeezed on and the car, in the proper attitude and proper line, accelerates out of the turn.

Type I Turn. A Type I turn is one that leads onto a straightaway. In this type of turn you brake early, get on the throttle just as early as possible, make a late apex and accelerate onto the following straight at maximum rate of speed. In the illustration below, it is put together like this:
1. *Maximum braking.*
2. *Braking almost complete, downshifted to lowest gear that will be used in accelerating out of turn.*
3. *Balancing point. Transition from braking to accelerating. This is a critical point. If you accelerate too early, you will have to let off to keep from running out of road on exit from turn. If you wait too long to begin acceleration, you will not be able to make entrance onto straight at maximum speed.*
4. *Late apex. Should be at or very nearly at full throttle.*
5. *Full throttle, accelerating at maximum rate.*
6. *Full throttle, clear of turn, using all of the road to make a smooth arc on to straightaway.*

*Type II Turn. A Type II turn is one that comes at the end of a straight-
away. In order to get maximum benefit from straightaway speed, brake as
late as possible, take an early apex, continue braking into turn and position the car for whatever comes next on the course.*
1. *Delay braking just as late as possible, using fixed reference point to begin braking.*
2. *Early apex, braking slightly less in this area as you begin to steer the
   car into the turn.*
3. *Lighter braking (and possibly sliding) as you widen the radius of the
   turn.*
4. *Balancing point. Transition to very light throttle to "set" car on
   suspension.*
5. *Sufficient throttle to properly line up for next portion of the course.*

If a driver has to lift off the gas during the exit from a Type I
turn to keep from running off the outside edge of the road, he
has done one or more of the following things wrong—braked
too late, made his apex too early, began accelerating too soon,
or applied too much gas too soon. This has to be worked on to
get it just right, but this is where the big payoff is—this is where
you can really pick up time.

TYPE II TURN

A Type II turn, the second most important type of turn on
the race track, is one that comes at the end of a straightaway.
Races are won on the straight, remember? So when the driver

has gotten onto the straightaway as fast as possible and gone down that straight at as high a speed as his car will take him, what he wants to do is get the benefit of this speed just as long as possible. So in a Type II turn, he brakes late. As late as he possibly can and still make the turn. He shouldn't be concerned about shifting down or when he's going to accelerate again. He should worry about going just as deep as he can without running out of road.

Braking for a Type II turn is a fine art. When a car is going in a straight line, the driver can apply full brakes, using enough pedal pressure to achieve maximum deceleration short of sliding the tires. A sliding tire has less adhesion than a rolling tire, so tires shouldn't slide. The pressure on the brake pedal should be modulated to keep just short of skidding, but don't pump the brakes just to be pumping them.

It is also possible to continue braking while steering into the turn but when this is done, the pressure on the pedal must be decreased because then the tires are developing slip from the

Compound turn with examples of Type II (coming off straight), Type III (turn between turns) and Type I (leading onto straight) turns.
1. *Delay braking just as late as possible.*
2. *Early apex, slightly less braking as car begins to turn.*
3. *Balancing point, using very slight amount of throttle to "set" car.*
4. *Hold light throttle, follow smooth radius, not trying to go too fast.*
5. *Still light throttle, being especially careful to stay to inside of course and not increase acceleration too soon as this will carry you to outside of course and spoil exit.*
6. *Balancing point. Car should be lined up for exit and beginning to accelerate.* ·
7. *Hard acceleration, very nearly full throttle.*
8. *Late apex, full throttle, enter straight at maximum acceleration and use all of road getting onto straight at fastest possible speed.*

turning forces on them and the combined forces of braking and turning result in a reduction of adhesion. Progressively, the more sharply the wheels are turned, the less braking can be applied without skidding.

In a Type II turn an early apex is used, only about a third to a half of the way around the radius of the turn. At this point the driver will still be braking, though much more lightly than earlier, and he may or may not have shifted down, depending on what he has to do next.

Some courses have one long continuous turn between two straights—such as Riverside's turn 9, or turn 2 at Daytona. Some of these start out as Type II turns and then change to a Type I before the other straight. On other turns that connect two straights there may not be a Type II turn at all but simply a Type I. Where this happens, a Type I turn always takes priority and if it can be driven as *either* a Type I or a Type II, it should *always* be treated as a Type I. Even where there is a long turn, the driver should not allow the late-braking approach to the Type II turn to interfere with being set up properly for the Type I turn that follows. A Type I turn is *always* more important.

TYPE III TURN

For a Type III turn, which is one that connects two or more other turns, the rule is this: Don't try to go too fast. It is the least important type of turn on the race track. What is impor-

Doing it wrong in the Type III portion of a compound turn. Driver made proper approach through Type II portion of turn (1-3) but started acceleration too soon (4-5), which pushed him too far to the outside of the turn. This causes him to have to get off throttle (6) to stay on road before he can begin acceleration again (7). He should have kept speed down (5), stayed on inside of turn in order to have been lined up for maximum-speed acceleration through Type I turn onto following straight.

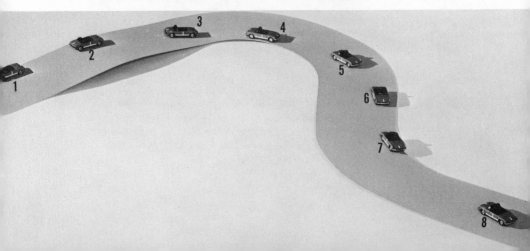

Doing it wrong in a Type I turn. A typical example of what can happen if you delay braking too long, get on wrong line and are going too fast entering a Type I turn.

1. *Car 1 is on correct line, has completed braking and has car balanced, almost ready to start acceleration. Car 5 has nosed ahead, braking late going into turn.*
2. *Car 1, still on right line, not letting presence of other car distract him from his own driving pattern, is making late apex, nearly at full throttle. Car 5's momentum has carried him to outside after the apex of the turn and even at this point he is still unable to apply full throttle.*
3. *Car 1, still under full acceleration, has made much faster entrance onto straight and is past Car 5 and pulling away. Car 5 has had to let off to stay on road and is still getting straightened around.*

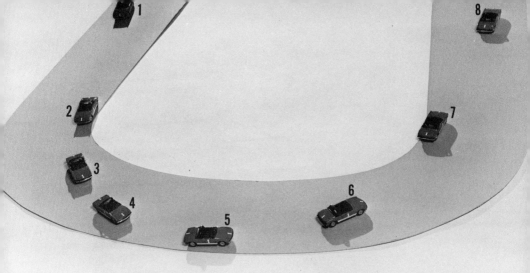

Compound turn that is a typical example of a Type II turn that leads to a Type I turn. Here you brake late coming into the Type II turn, then balance car and get set early for maximum-speed acceleration on to straight that follows.
1. *Delay braking just as late as possible.*
2. *Early apex.*
3. *Lighter braking as car begins to turn.*
4. *Balancing point. Transition to light throttle to "set" car.*
5. *Apply enough throttle to set up for exit.*
6. *Acceleration.*
7. *Late apex. Now under full throttle.*
8. *Exit turn, using all of road onto straightaway at maximum rate of acceleration.*

tant in a Type III turn is getting set up on the right line for the Type I turn that inevitably has to follow.

It is astounding the number of drivers who will just burn up the track through a Type III turn, thinking to themselves, boy, am I eating up these guys in front of me. And then lose all the ground they gained, and more, because they weren't in the right line to make a maximum-speed entrance onto the next straight. I've known any number of drivers who are real tigers through the switchbacks. One and a half seconds a lap faster than anybody else through the turns, they say. And maybe they are. But inevitably, as you come to the Type I turn leading onto the straight, there they are, completely in the wrong line, in the wrong gear, still braking and scratching. And when everybody goes by on the straight they'll be thinking, Wow, if I only had that kind of power I'd show these guys.

So for a Type III turn, the driver should take it easy and get set for the Type I that has to be ahead. For every second gained in a Type II turn, you'll lose two later if you're out of shape for the Type I that follows.

PRIORITIES

When a driver has completed his analysis of a circuit, he should know which turns are the most important and which he's going to concentrate on. The Type I turn leading onto the longest straight is the most important turn on any race track. Then the one leading onto the next-longest straight, and so on.

When he has gotten all the Type I turns down pat, then and only then should he go on to concentrate on the Type II turns. Here he'll be working on braking points, finding out how deep he can go and also looking for some fixed point he can use as a reference for braking at the same place every time.

To enable yourself to learn and continue to follow the proper line and to brake and accelerate at the proper spot you need points of orientation. In selecting these, never pick anything that can move. Use a mark on the pavement, trees, large rock, but never a turn worker or even a rubber cone.

Ontario's road course is one of the most difficult to orient yourself on because for safety reasons everything is moved back away from the track. At one very important spot on the track where I set up for the turn leading onto the infield straight I use a little wiggle in the white line on the right side of the course to set up and begin acceleration. It's such a small wiggle I need help to find it so I wait till the main grandstand lines up just right then look for my wiggle. Without it I can't get through this turn at maximum speed.

Finally, you should study the Type III turns and use those only to get into the best possible position for the following Type I turn and your entry onto the next straight.

But most of all you should work on Type I turns and always

Doing it wrong in the same turn. Doing it this way, the driver is not able to make a proper late-braking entrance into Type II turn or get onto the following straight at maximum acceleration through the Type I turn. Compare this with the right line shown in previous example.

keep in mind that races are won—and lost—on the straightaways, and that straightaway speeds depend on how you drive
Type I turns.

UPHILL & DOWNHILL

The uphill and downhill portions of any racing circuit have a
great effect on the acceleration, deceleration and turning of any
car. The skillful competition driver uses these to his advantage—and conversely, attempts to minimize their disadvantages.

First of all, a car going uphill has more adhesion than a car
going downhill. Going uphill, the car is "heavier," the inertia of
the forward motion tends to press it down onto the road and
the brakes are more effective. Going downhill the opposite is
true; the car is "lighter" and the brakes less effective.

Taking the same situation and putting a turn in it, as race
course designers often do, it's easy to see that on an uphill turn
the car has much better traction than in a turn of the same
radius going downhill. Even more complex are those turns that
have a hill in the middle where you start out going uphill into
the turn, continue over the crest and then go downhill, still
turning.

Riverside's turn 7, where there's a hill just before the turn, is
a Type II turn, one where you brake late. Coming up the hill,
the brakes go full on. But because the turn isn't until the bottom of the hill on the other side, it's also necessary to brake on
the downhill side. This requires three separate phases to the
braking pattern. First, going uphill, the brakes go full on, taking
advantage of the weight of the car being pressed down onto the
road. Second, at the crest of the hill, the brakes are almost
completely off; otherwise all four wheels will lock as the car
goes over the top and becomes light. And third, when the car
comes down, the weight back on the tires again, a little more
braking can be applied. If you measured the braking force in
these three phases, they might read something like this: Uphill,
100 percent; Crest, 10 percent; Downhill, 50 percent, then
dropping off again as the car is turned into turn 7. Another
complication is that you begin to turn before you're off the
brake.

Let's take some examples. Laguna Seca has several good
ones. There's a high-speed left bend just beyond the pits that
crests a hill. There's a lefthander that is strictly uphill onto an
uphill straight. And there's a corkscrew at the top that is level
going in but falls off sharply into a left and a right and then into
a left hand downhill sweeper. Riverside's turn 7 is a prize ex-

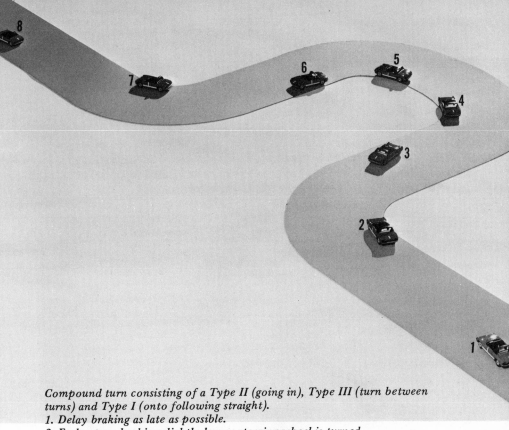

Compound turn consisting of a Type II (going in), Type III (turn between turns) and Type I (onto following straight).

1. *Delay braking as late as possible.*
2. *Early apex, braking slightly less as steering wheel is turned.*
3. *Braking finished, very light throttle, car balanced.*
4. *Maintain very light throttle, staying to inside of course.*
5. *Still very light throttle, following inside line. Too much throttle here and position 4 would force car to outside, making it impossible to be in perfect position for the Type I turn that follows.*
6. *Begin acceleration as turn opens up.*
7. *Late apex, full throttle.*
8. *On to straight at maximum acceleration, using all of road.*

ample of a hill toward the end of a straight where there is an uphill section where the brakes work extremely well, then a crest and a very short downhill section as the road turns into an off-camber (the outside of the turn being lower than the inside) lefthander. At Sears Point Raceway north of San Francisco there's a downhill turn called the carousel where the radius is constant and the car slides very easily. At Seattle International Raceway the next-to-last turn goes left while cresting the top of a hill and this makes the car lift and it is consequently very easy to slide at that point.

In order to use the uphill and downhill portions of the circuit to his advantage, the driver has to feel what's going on with the car. In the uphill left bend at Laguna Seca, for instance, the

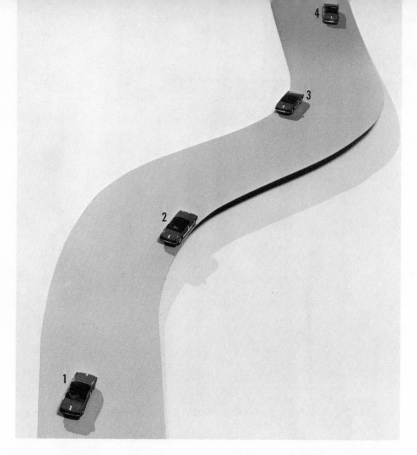

*Typical "ess" bend. Although this may look like it can be driven in a
straight line, there are two critical points to keep in mind. First, as this
bend leads onto another straight, it should be regarded as a Type I turn.
Therefore you have to plan ahead in order to get onto the following
straight at maximum speed.*

*1. Speed here should be such that the ess bend can be taken at full throttle,
or very near full throttle. This may require lifting off throttle or even
braking lightly before this point.*

2. Line up the two turns and use all of course making this apex.

3. Apex on other side of course. Full acceleration.

4. Exit on to following straightaway, full acceleration, using all of road.

Can-Am cars are fast enough that most drivers ease back on the
throttle just a hair to avoid too much lift, then continue their
acceleration. The uphill lefthander going onto the short uphill
straight on the back of the course, a Type I turn, is a place to
set up early and really pour it on. The car is heavy here, pressed
down onto the road, and sticks like glue. At the top, still going
slightly uphill, it is necessary to get all the braking done early
because the corkscrew is all downhill. Through the lefthander
past the crest a very light foot is required because it's also
slightly off-camber, as well as being downhill, but the right-

hander that follows is slightly banked so the car gets heavy again and it's possible to accelerate downhill toward the sweeper that follows. Through the sweeper it is necessary to feather the throttle, playing a delicate balance because this is also downhill and inertia would like to make the car slide off the outside of the turn.

The constant-radius downhill turn through the carousel at Sears Point follows another turn and then leads onto a straight so it could be described as a Type III turn that leads to a Type I turn. Because it is downhill, the car is light and will slide much more easily than it would in a turn of the same radius on level ground. So through most of the carousel, the wise thing to do is not try to go too fast but concentrate on making the perfect exit from the turn and enter the straight that follows exactly right. The road flattens out at the bottom of the carousel and the driver can take advantage of this by pouring on the throttle as the car gets heavy. This can be overdone, however, as the car is still turning as it hits bottom and will be jostled a car-width or two to the outside as it goes onto level ground again.

The next-to-last turn at Seattle, which turns left while cresting a hill, is between two straights but as a Type I turn takes priority over a Type II turn, this should be driven like a Type I. So the driver should brake early, take a late apex and get set for the short straight that follows. If he tries to brake late, as he would for a Type II turn, he'll find himself running out of road and not be set to make a proper maximum-speed entrance onto the next straight.

All this uphill-downhill theory can also be experienced in everyday driving. You can convince yourself how much better your brakes work going uphill than downhill. And with any luck, you can also find a deserted road someplace out of town where you can learn about uphill and downhill turns and the effect they have on the adhesion of your car.

ESSES

On some circuits there is a series of continuous shallow bends and these are usually called the esses. Some of these, especially if they're too sharp, become a series of Type III turns between turns and are largely meaningless in terms of lap times for slower cars but can be very important for faster cars. In such esses as these all the driver can normally do is play follow-the-leader and wait for the turn that leads onto the straight that comes at the other end. Other esses, like those between turns 1 and 6 at Riverside, can be interesting and challenging. On these

77

the driver has to get a feeling for what's going on, what's coming next and which is the best part of the road to use. Ordinarily, the best practice is to try to straighten them out as much as possible (you can always go faster in a straight line than sideways) and then get slowed down early and into the proper line for the Type I turn that comes at the end. Occasionally, by changing his line slightly, he can pick off another driver if the other driver isn't being alert. This usually happens early in the race when the cars tend to bunch together and slow down, accordion fashion, to play follow-the-leader.

A single S-shaped bend or a chicane that breaks up a long straight is a classic example of all three types of turns: Down the straight into a Type II turn, through the wiggle-woggle of a Type III turn and then a Type I turn leading onto the next straight. Turns 7 and 7A on Riverside's short course are typical. You come onto the straightaway at turn 6 (Type I) and go down the straight to turn 7 as fast as possible. The driver brakes hard as he goes uphill, lets off as he tops the rise, then applies a little more braking as the car becomes balanced again. He starts turning left, easing off the brakes as he turns, taking an early apex. At about this point he is entering the Type III portion of turn 7-7A. He could get over onto the straight much more quickly by straightening out the ess but that would spoil his

perfect entrance onto the backstretch. So he shifts down, swings to the left, getting to the outside of the turn to start his acceleration as soon as possible to make a late apex and accelerate onto the backstretch.

WATCH CAREFULLY

It is important for the driver to drive his own race. Learning by following is much overrated as a way to learn. The driver should establish his own braking points, his own places for opening the throttle, his own shift points and his own apexes. Admittedly, there are times when it is valuable to follow another driver and study his driving pattern. It may reveal a weak spot that will enable a more alert driver to pass him. But don't follow another driver and make the mistake of driving his race instead of your own.

It is important, however, to observe other drivers at work, especially those who are obviously the best at the job. I remember watching Bruce McLaren and Denis Hulme during the first practice session for the Can-Am at Riverside in 1968. It was a revelation to me to see how expert they were at their jobs. I think I may have been most impressed by their knowing where to go slow or, to put it another way, where it wasn't important to go fast. I watched them from turn 8, up at the head of the straight on Riverside's long course, as they perfected their entrance onto the backstretch. Before very many laps had passed they had it down to an exact science and I could see that they were using the slight uphill stretch entering turn 8 for their heaviest braking getting into the turn (Type II), then taking it easy around most of the turn (Type III), getting set at exactly the right place and accelerating out onto the backstretch in one smooth, continuous arc (Type I). The level of driving skill in Can-Am racing is pretty high but there were still some drivers who were trying to go fast through the middle part of turn 8 and consequently they were sliding, getting sideways and having a terrible time. But not Bruce and Denny, they drove through most of turn 8 as if it weren't important at all (which it isn't), and when the time came, they went onto that backstretch like they'd been fired from cannons.

There are lots of fine points in racing. Some of them we'll talk about later, others you'll pick up yourself as you gain experience. You should perfect the basic driving techniques first, though, and not be too impatient to break the rules. If you take care of learning the basics, the fine points will take care of themselves.

Putting it All Together

A LOT OF THE INFORMATION in the preceding chapters has been about things to do on the race track and it may be difficult to see how they all fit together. So let me try to describe the way I go about learning a circuit when I race on it for the first time.

For this example, let's use Road Atlanta. It's the home of the American Road Race of Champions and one of the most challenging circuits in the country to get just right.

Long before going to Atlanta for the 1970 ARRC I obtained a course diagram and got a pretty good idea of the general layout. I supplemented this by talking to Dan Parkinson, who had already raced there, and by carefully reading a report on the circuit in *Autoweek* written by Bob Sharp. Both of these drivers have been National Champions and I respect their opinions. So when I arrived at Road Atlanta, I had a fairly clear picture of what the course was like. I had also made mental notes about the turns I felt would be the most important ones to learn and the sequence in which I would try to learn them.

Before going out on the course for the first time in my racing car, my teammate and I had the opportunity to go around the course in a rental car. We did this at a very easy pace, taking a close look at the circuit. I studied it carefully, observing the uphills and downhills, and also took care to note the areas off at the sides of the circuit. I especially noted those areas where there was something that could cause a problem if I got off course, saying to myself, "There's a healthy embankment, don't get off the course here." Or, in a safer spot, "Even if I do have to get off course here I can straighten it out and get back on without trouble." I also studied the composition of the surface where dirt had been washed across it and would cause that part to be a little more slippery. And I looked carefully at the places where there might be more wear and tear in the groove, causing the course to be rougher, or where oil would likely be dropped, causing the course to be slick.

After having this look at the course from the rental car, it was then easy to go through my procedure for classifying the various corners into Type I, II and III turns.

At Road Atlanta, as on all road circuits, the most important turn on the course is the turn leading onto the longest straight. This is turn 7 (see map) and it is followed by a straight that is nearly a mile long for the kind of car I was driving. The Group 7 cars that run at Road Atlanta for the Can-Am would have to back off toward the end of the straight for a downhill bend but in my car, a Porsche 914/6, I was not having to lift for this. So I noted turn 7 down as the top priority turn on the circuit.

The next most important turn on any course is that preceding the next-longest straight. At Road Atlanta, this is turn 5. The third priority turn is that preceding the next-longest straight. And this is turn 11, the one before the start-finish straight. There is effectively a little straight section that follows turn 3, so this is a Type I turn as well.

Next I studied the Type II turns, those that come at the end of straight sections. At Road Atlanta, in order of importance, these are turn 10 (the longest straight), turn 6 (the next-longest

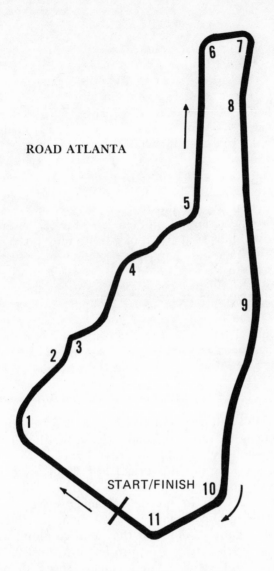

ROAD ATLANTA

START/FINISH

straight), and turn 1 (the start-finish straight).

As for Type III turns, which are those that come between two other turns, there is one at Road Atlanta that is an excellent example of a Type III turn because it is unimportant in terms of making time but very important in terms of not going too fast. This is Turn 2. Turns 8 and 9 at Road Atlanta are merely sweeping bends in the straightaway and are not turns that have to be learned in the same way as the others. On those you just hang on and go as fast as you can. Turn 4 is also a Type III turn—and it's a different sort of Type III. We'll talk about it later.

83

Even a small incline that flattens out, as does this one a

Even though I had prepared myself as well as I could before I drove my racing car around Road Atlanta for the first time, I was still surprised by a couple of areas. I took it easy the first couple laps, checking out the ideas I had about the course and this is always a good idea because lots of things change on the circuit as you get up to speed. At racing speed, changes in elevation, banking and camber have much more effect on the car. Turn 2 is a good example of this. You go uphill in turn 1, then the road levels out as you turn left into turn 2. This is a much more abrupt termination at racing speed than it is at rental-car speed and the effect on the car is considerable. If you're not prepared for it, you can go straight on off the course. Also, because the car gets light there if you're not lined up exactly right coming over the hill, you won't be able to brake sufficiently to make turn 3. And as turn 3 is a Type I turn, you want to be in exactly the right place to make your entrance onto the straight that follows at maximum speed.

Another place I found to be very interesting was the bend at the bottom of the hill at the end of the back straight. This bend is not numbered on the course map. When I first drove through it I felt that I would not be able to go through it without lifting

d Atlanta, can cause car to get "light" and reduce traction.

as you're really going fast there and I felt the car would simply slide off the road. Nevertheless, because it is flattening out at the bottom of the hill, the car is very heavy there and sticks better than you think it will. So I found out that by trying a little more and a little more and a little more I was able to get through this bend at top speed.

But back to our learning process. I concentrated first on turn 7. This is a rather simple turn to learn as it is slightly banked and this enables you to get good traction through the turn. The important thing here, as in all Type I turns, is to begin your acceleration as early as possible. To line up properly for this turn you have to go back to turn 6 and be sure that you don't get out of shape too much there so as to be in the proper line and going slowly enough to begin your acceleration early going into turn 7. Then you can shoot out onto the straightaway going like gangbusters and have that speed up all the way down that long straight.

Turn 5, which is the corner preceding the next-longest straight and hence our second priority in learning the course, is the turn that follows the esses. It is a little tricky for that reason because the esses essentially constitute a straight section of road where you can go flat out. Thus you may make the mistake of thinking that turn 5 is a Type II turn at the end of a straight, one where you brake late. But you should think of it as a Type I, remembering that if you can treat it as a Type I or a Type II turn, always regard it as a Type I. So approaching turn 5 you brake early, get your acceleration started early and use that maximum speed just as long as possible going down the straight toward turn 6.

Turn 11 is somewhat similar. This is a sweeping turn to the right that precedes the start-finish straight. Here you come down the hill from turn 10 and you can go into the turn so fast that you can't get all the way through without having to back off. So you need to slow down early so you can accelerate all the way through the turn and thereby maintain as high a speed as possible all the way down the start-finish straight.

Turn 3, the hard righthander at the top of the hill, is also a Type I turn since the esses leading up to turn 5 are essentially a straight that you can drive through at full speed. With a faster car, you will be sliding but you can achieve high speed through here if you're in exactly the right line and make a proper entrance. So regard turn 3 as a Type I turn, one that leads onto a straight, not a Type III turn-between-turns as you might think from the map.

The Type II turn that is of first priority is the turn that follows the longest straight and at Road Atlanta that is turn 10. You come down the long straight, the road bends to the right, goes downhill, then there's an abrupt uphill turn to the left. This is the turn mentioned earlier where I thought at first it would be impossible to go through at full speed but later discovered that I could. After the dip you're beginning to go uphill so the traction is very good both for turning and braking. And on this uphill portion you must brake immediately since turn 10 is a blind corner. That is, you have to brake and get set for it before you can actually see it. Turn 10 goes to the right under the bridge and when you crest the top of the hill you must be slowed down enough so you don't slide off the road into the bank on the left side. There is plenty of time following turn 10 to set up properly for turn 11, so you can concentrate fully on getting as deeply into turn 10 as possible before braking. So in turn 10 you put a couple of basic principles to work for you. As it is a Type II turn, one where you brake as late as possible, you go flat out just as long as possible, then use the uphill portion to help improve the effectiveness of your braking.

86   Turn 6, the next-priority Type II turn, is somewhat similar.

This follows the straight from turn 5 and it also is a turn where you can brake very late because it has a slight banking and this enables you to go a little further into the turn than you would if it were a flat, unbanked turn. You can go into this turn very deep and still maintain a good line and be in the proper shape to shut down and get set for turn 7, the most important turn on the course.

Turn 1 is also an interesting Type II turn where you can brake very late. This is probably the best place on the course to pass another car since you can get into the turn quite a bit deeper than you really need to before you brake because it starts uphill as it turns and your car consequently has better traction. So you can stay off the gas, dive inside, then use the hill to slow yourself down. Turn 1 is another of those turns where you should concentrate on braking and use your last possible braking point.

At Road Atlanta, the most important Type III turn, one of those that comes between two other turns, is turn 2. This is a turn that you definitely do not want to go through too fast. You come uphill from turn 1, then the hill levels off and the road goes to the left. At this point you could stay on the gas across the top of the hill and get through turn 2 more quickly. But if you do this, your chances of staying on the course are not very good. What you need to do is slow down early so that you are properly lined up to take turn 3, a Type I turn, which is much more important in terms of lap speed.

Turn 4 is also a Type III turn-between-turns. This is at the bottom of the hill in the esses and what you need to do here is make sure you go through in the proper line. It is pretty much a flat-out turn (all Type III turns aren't slow turns) but you must be in the proper line in order to take turn 5 properly. And turn 5, you'll remember, is the second-most important turn on the course as it leads onto the second-longest straight.

Okay, those are the turns at Road Atlanta, the order of their importance and the order in which I concentrated on learning them. Now let's put it all together and take a fast lap of the circuit.

Going down the start-finish straight, I'm in fourth gear and on this stretch, if I'm being pushed, I can leave it in fourth all the way to the other end. If I'm not being pushed, I shift into fifth gear about 200 ft. before I have to brake in order to keep the revs down and take as little out of the engine as possible. My braking point is just at the re-entry road from the pits on the left side and there I get on the brakes hard. Here I cock the car just slightly, forcing it to lean into the hill in Turn 1, shift back to third gear and then get on the gas as early as possible, squeezing it on as it will take it going up the hill. Going up the hill the car is rather heavy so it sticks well and I can really fly up that hill. At the same time, I'm moving to the righthand side of the road just as quickly as I can. About three-fourths of the way up the hill I begin turning to the left so as not to take the leveling off at the top of the hill too abruptly, which would cause the car to bounce up on the suspension and throw it out of balance more than is necessary. I smooth out turn 2 as much as possible and as soon as the car settles after the rise, I'm on the brakes as hard as possible without sliding and shifting down to second gear to take turn 3. Turn 3, which is a Type I turn, is one where you want to begin your acceleration before the apex but in turn 3, you must also be aware that you have to be in the right line for turn 4. What you have to do is put all these turns together through the esses so that when you come to turn 5, you're in the right spot to brake early and get ready to shoot out onto the straight.

You have to be careful in turn 5, it's one of the places that drivers get into trouble at Road Atlanta if they leave their braking too late. I found in turn 5 that I could get on the throttle early and if I was a shade too fast I could drop a wheel off into the dirt coming out without hurting my speed up the straight. So about one out of three laps, I would just touch the dirt on the right side after the exit, using up all the course and a little more, making the best possible speed down to turn 6.

Going down the straightaway to turn 6 I work up to fifth gear again, then brake very hard and very late. Because this corner is banked, it is possible to begin turning into the corner before completing the braking. In this particular corner I found that it was better only to go back to third gear as this was a little faster than dropping back to second and then having to shift up to third and back to second again for turn 7.

Approaching turn 7 I brake just a shade on the early side and shift down to second a little early too in order to have the power on early, and be able to accelerate through turn 7 as quickly as possible in the proper line. This is also a banked turn, which gives good traction, and I shift back up to third almost before I am all the way out of the turn, using up all the road, then working up to fifth down the straight. The tachometer in my car is reading about 8000 rpm at the top of the hill at the other end of the straight but I'm not sure what it reads at the bottom of the hill because my attention is absolutely demanded going through the bend at the bottom.

Immediately after the bump at the bottom I get on the brakes hard, letting the hill help slow the car, back to fourth, back to third, then across the hill under the bridge, turn 10. Going into this turn it is important to fight the car because it wants to go to the right side of the road under braking. And what you have to do is bring it to the left side of the road so you line up properly through turn 10. Turn 10 is a potential problem turn because you have to be in the right line going through the turn or otherwise you won't be able to stay on the road as the car gets light when you go over the top of the hill. Past the bridge on the left side is the exit to the pits and I found that I could use part of that exit road and still get back to line up for the next turn without going off the road.

Next comes turn 11 and it is very important to be in good position to take it just right. Turn 11 may be the most deceptive turn on the course. I was using third gear there when I started out in practice and by the time we raced, I was well up into fourth gear. So it's a great deal faster than it looks. It's also an important turn, the third most important turn on the course.

Coming out of turn 11 in fourth gear it is easy to have a look at the starter and then immediately to look for my pit board. The location of the pits at Road Atlanta, immediately on the left side of the start-finish straight, is a very easy place from which to see a pit board.

So that's Road Atlanta. A much more challenging course than most. One that combines pretty nearly every condition you'll ever encounter on a road circuit—except a 180-degree airport type turn. You use every gear from second to fifth, you have to use your brakes where they'll do the most good, there are changes in elevation that work both for you and against you, there is a fast section where you can go at maximum speed for considerable time, yet it's one of the safest courses I've ever driven on.

Most road circuits aren't as difficult to learn because they don't contain so many challenges but I think that if you are one of those drivers who really learns Road Atlanta, you'll be able to go fast anywhere.

AIRPORT CIRCUITS

While we're talking about learning race courses, let's use a couple more examples. Airport circuits, though becoming few and far between, present an interesting learning challenge although they can be learned much more quickly and consequent-

ly enable you to work up to your maximum lap speed more easily. On an airport circuit there are usually only two kinds of turns, a 90-degree turn and a 180-degree turn, but we can apply the same system of priorities to an airport course.

For this example, let's use Holtville Airbase International Raceway (HAIR), an abandoned airstrip in the Imperial Valley east of San Diego. From the start-finish straight you go down to turn 1, a 180-degree righthander that is rather wide and has a weathered concrete surface. As this is followed by another straight, you consider this a Type I turn, one where you brake early, get on the gas early, make a late apex and accelerate out using every inch of the road. At the end of this straight is a chicane consisting of a turn to the left, a turn to the right, another turn to the right and then another turn to the left which puts you back on the same straightaway as before. As you enter the chicane you drive it as a Type II turn (brake late), the middle part is Type III (turns between turns) and as you come out it is a Type I (onto a straight).

Going on down to turn 5 at the other end of the course you have a duplication of turn 1, a simple 180-degree right hand bend. This is followed by another straight so it is a Type I turn

where you brake early, get on the gas early, take a late apex and use up all the road coming out. Coming back down the course you have another chicane, this one a little more extended, but it is very much the same as the one you encountered before. Going into it you brake as late as possible (Type II), don't go too fast through the middle (Type III) so as to be lined up properly to come out onto the next straight as fast as possible (Type I). This puts you onto the start-finish straight and you're ready to go around again.

There isn't nearly as great a challenge from an airport circuit, as I said before; nevertheless there are certain things you should be aware of and watch for on such circuits. Changes in road surface are very common on old airbases—concrete, old concrete, new blacktop and old blacktop. These have different adhesion characteristics so that some portions will be stickier than others. It is also likely to break up in places, turning everything into marbles, and your tire wear may be very high. It is important to watch for pylons that are knocked down, too, not only to avoid running over them and perhaps damaging your car but also because you may be able to shorten up the course, use more of the road and make faster lap times.

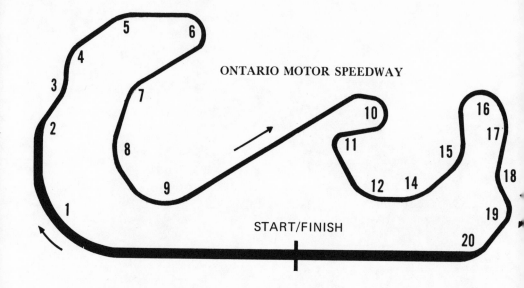

ONTARIO MOTOR SPEEDWAY

START/FINISH

ONTARIO MOTOR SPEEDWAY

The road circuit at Ontario Motor Speedway presents still
another kind of challenge to the driver as it is different in
different ways than either the Road Atlanta or the Holtville
type of courses. At Ontario the road circuit uses part of the
2½-mile oval as the straightaway and the rest of it wiggles
through the infield. There are no elevation changes and the
turns are arbitrarily arranged in what the designer thought
would make a challenging circuit. One of the characteristics at
Ontario is that there is almost nothing located close to the
course by which you can orient yourself and thereby know exactly where you are at any given moment. This makes it a very
safe course since there's nothing to run into but it also makes it
difficult to learn and difficult to drive consistently.

Let's take a lap at Ontario and analyze the circuit as we go.
On the straightaway past the pits all road racing cars get up to
their maximum speed and the first turn (which is the last turn
on the oval because the Indy cars go the other way) is flat out
for everybody and should be considered as part of the straight.
But as you come down off the oval onto the road course, you
are immediately faced by an extremely interesting series of
high-speed bends. For turn 2 you simply line up properly in
turn 1 so you can go through it as fast as possible. In my
Porsche, it's necessary to feather the throttle just a little bit.

Approaching turn 3, you have to brake early so that you come through it tight to the inside and that helps you line up for turn 4. Then you accelerate as hard as you can, going flat out through turn 4 and probably turn 5, then brake early going into turn 6. Again, the way you take turn 5 will depend to some extent on the kind of car you're driving. You may have to feather the throttle there too, to stay on the road.

Turn 6 is followed by a straight so it is a Type I turn where you brake early, accelerate early, make a late apex and head for turn 7 going as fast as possible. You straighten out turn 7 as much as you can, the same for turn 8, letting off a little bit through turn 8 in order to be properly lined up for turn 9. Because there are no reference points here, it is extremely difficult to get this turn exactly right and in a previous chapter I described how I found my wiggly white line on the outside of the course between 8 and 9 so as to line up properly. Turn 9 is a Type I turn, the second most important turn on the course because it precedes the 2nd-longest straight. By finding my reference point I am able to hit the apex at turn 9 just right and use every inch of the road as I start down the infield straight. If you miss this point—and that's easy to do in the heat of battle—it spoils your line, you have to brake later and that spoils your entrance onto the straight.

Turn 10 is a Type II turn, one where you brake late and continue braking as you go through the first part of the turn. It's important here, although you're trying to make good time through turn 10, that you stay to the right side of the course so you can smooth out turn 11 as much as possible. If you don't, you'll have to slow down a lot more and instead of a smooth, continuous ess into turn 11 you'll have to slow down, then make a hard right and a hard left and lose a lot of time.

Turns 11, 12, 13 and 14 are a series of lefthand bends so you go through them as fast as possible, and as smoothly as possible, but not so fast through 13 and 14 that you get into turn 15 going too fast. Turn 15 is another Type I turn with a very short straight leading down to 16 so you want to get onto it in good shape to take advantage of that as much as you can.

Turn 16 is one of those turns which you can get into too fast and thereby lose time. So it is important in 16 to stay to the inside and watch for the turn to open up so you are properly lined up to take advantage of the straight between turns 16 and 18. So remember that turn 16, although it comes at the end of a straight, should be treated as a Type I turn because it leads onto another straightaway. Turn 17, in case you missed it, is a jog

93

through which you can go at full acceleration and doesn't need any special notice.

Turn 18 is one that needs to be taken with a great deal of care so as not to be out of shape for the most important turn on the course, turn 19, the turn preceding the longest straight. So you brake hard into turn 18 and stay on the left side of the course down to turn 19. Turn 19 is a very tight righthand bend and although it is simple to negotiate, you have to be sure that you brake early, get on the gas early and come through turn 20 and onto the straight accelerating just as hard as you can. And there you are going past the pits again. Okay?

Now, let me ask you how you would go about learning the Ontario road circuit. What turns do you regard as most important and in what sequence would you learn them?

First, of course, is turn 19, the Type I turn leading onto the longest straight (turn 20 being taken at full acceleration). That's first priority. The infield straight after turn 9 is the next-longest straight and while that's also very important, I think I'd concentrate a little more on the series of turns from 1 through 5. Here you have to experiment, finding out what is going to be the right line in turn 1 so as to get through turn 2 as fast as possible. You also have to experiment with turn 3, discovering where you have to brake so as to be lined up so you can get through turn 4 in good shape. And when you're coming out of turn 4, you have to be lined up so as to get through turn 5 as fast as possible, finding out how much you have to get off the gas or whether you can go through there with your foot on the floor.

Maybe this series of turns is the exception that proves the rule about the sequence in which you learn a new circuit but on such a course as this, if you don't figure out how to get the best speed through this series of bends, you'll lose a lot of time.

After this I'd concentrate on turn 9, especially on finding a reference point to use, then turn 6, then turn 15, then turn 16. Those are all Type I turns.

Next I would concentrate on the Type II turns, those at the ends of the straightaways. We've already done the turns at the end of the longest straight, so I'd then work on turn 10, the turn at the end of the infield straight. And turn 10, believe it or not, is the only Type II turn at Ontario, the only one where you concentrate on braking late and going in as deeply as possible. All the other turns at the ends of straights lead to other straights and are therefore treated as Type I turns.

Last in the learning process, I'd work on the Type III turns, those that come between turns. These aren't unimportant but they are less important in terms of lap speed and the primary thing is to be sure that you don't drive so fast as to be out of shape and not able to take advantage of the Type I turn leading onto the next straightaway.

You can put these rules together learning any course and if you do, I know you'll have an advantage over the guy who just goes out and drives as hard as he can.

Strategies & Stratagems

IN A MILITARY SENSE, tactics are the individual actions taken to achieve an immediate objective while strategy is the overall game-plan intended to win the battle or the war. The same things are true in road racing. You use tactics to get ahead of another car and you employ strategy to win the race.

The basic tactic in road racing is to pass the car that is ahead of you. If you can do this, you've got a pretty fair advantage. But before we get into all this, I should point out that the basic rule of the road is that the overtaking car assumes all responsibility for avoiding contact. At the same time, it is also important to remember that any time your car gets bent, whether you were in the right or in the wrong, it's you and you alone that is going to stand the cost of having it fixed.

The best general advice I can offer about passing is for you to pass every car possible whenever you can do this without endangering either yourself or the other driver. Never willingly miss an opportunity to pass. Don't make the mistake of thinking you can do it next lap. Do it now. You have to use judgment and caution in this, of course, and early in your driving career you will lose positions because you hesitated when you should have moved. It takes experience to be able to judge just how much space it takes to get around another car, especially in a corner, and you have to work on this constantly to develop this knowledge.

The best—and safest—place to pass another car is on the straightaway. And this is also the easiest place to pass, provided you have the speed to accomplish it. Sometimes you will find that your car is a tiny little bit faster than your opponent's but not quite enough faster to let you get all the way around him on the straight. On the next lap you should try braking a little earlier for the Type I turn that leads onto the straight. This may give you just that little bit better shot out of the turn and enable you to gain those essential extra feet.

Slipstreaming down the straight is another technique that is sometimes successful in getting you around another car on the straight. When doing this, you follow in the "bubble" of air created by the other car and this makes it possible for you to achieve a higher rate of speed than you could if you were by yourself. When you're ready to make your move, you slide out around the car, smoothly but not too slowly, hoping that the extra momentum created when it was acting as your windbreak is sufficient to slingshot you past.

This technique is most successful with cars that are very evenly matched. You see it done in Formula Vee racing all the time and sometimes two or three or even four drivers will spend the whole race doing it to each other and everybody will be jockeying for the most advantageous position on the very last lap in the dash for the checkered flag. It is also common in stock car racing and many such races are won just this way between the last turn and the finish line.

There are three places where you can pass on a straightaway; coming out of the Type I turn at the beginning of the straight, in the middle of the straight when you go by on pure top speed, or by outbraking the other driver in the Type II turn at the other end of the straight.

When you are trying to get past your opponent on acceleration onto the straight, it is essential that you brake early, get the throttle on just as soon as possible, make a late apex and be in position to give it everything you've got as you enter the straight. Sometimes, by sitting right on his tailpipe, you can bug the other driver into delaying his braking too long. Then he won't be able to make a perfect entrance onto the straight and you can boom right on past him.

In a Type I turn, don't make the mistake of thinking you can pass him while he's still braking and beat him onto the straight. You may be able to get past temporarily but unless you make your perfect maximum-speed acceleration onto the straight, he'll come underneath you while you're still trying to get yourself underway again and you'll be even farther behind than you were before.

Outbraking another driver as you go into a Type II turn at the end of a straightaway not only takes good brakes but also requires a high degree of skill and judgment. Unless it puts you impossibly far off your line, try not to follow directly behind another car going into a Type II turn. This gives the other driver too much of an advantage as he can then brake early and keep the best line. If you're on the inside, he can't do anything except worry that you're going to outbrake him and this may cause him to make an error in judgment that will allow you to get past. As always, use your own braking point—the one you have found to be the latest place at which you can brake and still make the corner—and don't let your opponent dictate the tactics if you can avoid it.

A Type III turn between turns is not ordinarily a good place to pass another car but there are times when you may be able to take advantage of another driver there. It isn't going to do you any good to pass another driver in a Type III turn if it puts you out of position for the Type I turn ahead, though, so be sensible about it. But if you find a place where you can shoot past and then make it impossible for him to pass you, even though it spoils the perfect line for both of you, then it is worth it.

Esses are sometimes a good place to pass another driver if he isn't being alert to what's going on. Ordinarily you play follow-the-leader through the esses but once in a while you can figure out a tactic that will let you pass even where you wouldn't most of the time. At Riverside, for instance, you can sometimes pick off a driver going uphill to the entrance to turn 6 by planning well ahead, dropping back a little through the middle of the

esses, then building up more speed through the last part and squeaking past just before you have to brake and get set up for turn 6. Again, though, it's no good doing this if you have to brake so hard that you can't be on the right line for the corner and your rival simply accelerates past you through the Type I section of the turn.

Passing is one kind of tactic and keeping from being passed is another. When you're in the car ahead and another driver is on your tail and trying to get around you, then it's your job to make it just as difficult as possible without actually balking him. In a Type I turn there's only one "right" line for a maximum-speed entrance onto the straight so there you can brake even earlier than usual and he'll have to stay behind you if he's also going to make a proper entry. If he wants to try to shoot past you coming into the braking area, let him; that will spoil his line and you'll pass him on acceleration.

Going down the straight he may simply drive around you and, if he has the power to do this, there isn't much you can do to avoid it. If he tries to slingshot you on the straight, you can

sometimes bluff him out of it by staying to the inside or by
varying your line as you come down the straightaway. Naturally, you won't zig-zag down the straight to try to keep him
behind you, that would be unsportsmanlike and might get you
black-flagged besides.

At the other end of the straight coming to a Type II turn,
there are several tactics you can employ to keep from being
passed. The "right" line for a Type II turn isn't as clear-cut as
for a Type I turn, so you can use a variety of maneuvers that
may keep him behind you. In general, stay well to the inside of
the course, even though you have to brake earlier than usual. He
will also want that inside line going into a Type II turn and if
there's no room for him there, he will either have to stay behind
you or try to go around on the outside. Passing on the outside
in a turn is a tactic that Fangio was reported to be the master of
but in club racing where the cars and drivers are closely
matched, it's so rare as to be almost non-existent. In the early
part of your driving career, you'll get passed on the outside by
more experienced drivers but this will be because they will suck

you into braking too early. You'll think you have them safely bottled up behind you, then they'll go right on past on the outside, tuck in front of you, then brake hard and take the line into the corner, leaving you feeling foolish. What you should have done was brake on your own braking point and not let the other driver dictate the tactics.

After this has happened to you a few times you'll also learn to make it one of your own tactics for getting around an equally fast car. You follow him closely for several laps, letting him become confident that he can keep you behind. Then when he becomes used to you following him like a good boy, you zing past and do it to him.

Most of all, when another driver is trying to pass you, don't give him anything he can't take away from you. Even when he's got his nose up beside your door, don't let him fake you out. You may still be able to close the door on him if you take your normal line and make it plain to him that you're not going to yield to his pushy ways. He's in the overtaking car and it's his responsibility to avoid contact with you.

All these tactics we've been discussing apply only to those cars with which you are actually racing for position. If you're in a multiple-class race—and in club racing you'll be in a lot of these—you'll often be on the course with cars that are a lot faster than yours. When these come up to pass, you don't race with them; instead you make it just as easy as possible for them to pass so as not to interfere with their race. There's nothing that's quite so infuriating in club racing as coming up to pass a car in another class and having him want to dice with you.

So watch your rear-view mirror for a faster car that is coming up to pass, make it easy for him to get around you and when it will be a help to him, point to the side where you want him to pass. Don't change your line abruptly to get out of his way—that may be where he was intending to pass you—but do interfere with him just as little as possible.

STRATEGY

Because the average SCCA regional or national race is about 30 minutes long, you might think that your race strategy should be to go just as fast as your car will take you for the entire half hour. This is true only once in a very great while. The first few laps usually filter out quite a few cars; either the driver makes a mistake, spins and drops back, or something goes wrong with his car. My overall strategy for a 30-minute race is this: Get just as good a start as possible, pass every car I can during the all-out period in the early laps and then review my strategy to see what I should do for the rest of the race.

So the first priority is to get a good start. The cars immediately around you on the grid will be approximately the same speed as you; therefore, if you get hung up with a slightly slower car, the one that is the same speed as you will have a chance to get away. So a good start is essential. Pass every car you can whenever you can do it safely and don't give up a position if you can possibly avoid it.

Once the race has settled down, you should then apply the rules for turning in your fastest laps and begin working out the strategy for the rest of the race. At this point you will have shaken off the driver who was on your tailpipe and the one in front of you is far enough ahead that you have to settle down and do your best if you're going to catch him. This is the time to be super-precise in everything you do. This is where you really settle down to concentrate on driving those perfect laps. Smooth. Exact. Perfect. And you do it lap after lap after lap, each time striving to do it better, more smoothly, that little bit faster, take that corner a little more cleanly. If you're in front, this is the time to pull away. If you're behind, this is the time to close that gap.

This is also the time to study your opposition. Watch and see if there's a place on the course where your car is faster and try to figure out how you're going to get around him. Oftentimes two different types of cars will have the same overall lap times but one will be faster in one kind of turn while the other will have the advantage in another. I remember in the 1964 ARRC at Riverside I had a good dice with Dave Tallaksen when he was driving an Elva Courier and I was in my Speedster. We were almost exactly dead equal all the way around the course but his car was quicker through the esses and if he could have gotten around me, I'm sure that I could never have gotten past him again. What Dave should have done, I think, was to let me take my lead through the early part of the esses, then come through the last two bends at his full rate of speed and buzz past me going up the hill to turn 6. Luckily, for me, he never did this. Instead he would stay right on my tail all the way through the esses and this never allowed him to build up the speed that would have let him get past.

Another tactic that sometimes works when you're trying to get around another car is to act like he's holding you up—even though you're having all you can do just to catch up, never mind getting past. Feint at him where you can, make him shut the door on you, run up beside him on the outside going into a Type II turn, make him think you're going to try to tuck in front and outbrake him. Worry him in every way you can. You may be able to make him make the one mistake that will let you get ahead of him. But don't get yourself so far out of shape that you can't take advantage of the opportunity if he does get rattled and make that mistake.

This is the time to concentrate, concentrate, concentrate. Be aware of everything you do. Feel the car and know exactly how it is running. Often, if you are concentrating on your job, you can finish a race with a car that isn't running quite right. If your engine develops a miss at maximum rpm, then be aware of that and keep your revs just below that critical point, going just as fast as you can without getting into the ragged area. If your carburetion is a little off and the engine begins to starve on a long turn, be conscious of what's happening. When the engine starves it is running lean and that means you could burn a piston if you keep it up. Alter your line slightly, trying to find a way to get through the turn without the engine starving. Know what your oil temperature gauge says and if it begins to climb across the dial, try to figure out a way of stopping it. Sometimes it will help to "breathe" the engine on the straightaway, easing off the throttle for a moment, letting the engine get a slightly richer mixture to help cool the cylinders. But also concentrate on going just as fast as possible wherever you can. If you have to slow down, either because the engine won't live at maximum revs or because you're trying to save the car for a big push later, don't deliberately slow down but drop your rev limit and continue to concentrate on driving just as fast as you possibly can.

I remember an ARRC race at Riverside where I was driving as teammate to Milt Minter in a Porsche 911. When the race settled down after three or four laps, I was second behind Milt and I followed him lap after lap, concentrating just as hard as I could, figuring out my strategy and making it just as easy on my car as I could. I wasn't going to take any chances in trying to get past Milt, first of all. A 1-2 team finish, even if I didn't win, was what the team wanted, not a first with the other car off in the weeds someplace. If Bob Tullius hadn't come up and caught us three laps from the end, I would have followed Milt the whole way. But when Bob's Triumph came up on me and the three of us went into turn 9 together, I took that opportunity to go inside Milt and take the lead. Now it was my turn to increase my revs to the maximum and turn in the fastest possible laps. And because I had been saving my car—and also because I didn't let myself get hypnotized into following Milt, no matter what—I was able to put together these final laps and win the race.

Certainly my knowledge of the circuit helped me do this but most of all was that ability to concentrate when the pressure was on that got me home first. It's always a great feeling to win a national championship but this race, because my strategy paid off, was extra satisfying.

There will be times, of course, when all the strategy in the world won't do you any good. At the 1970 ARRC at Road Atlanta, for instance, my car had an intermittent miss in the fast bends that we were never able to solve and there was just no way my Porsche 914/6 could keep up with the Datsun 240Zs. In fact, I couldn't even keep up with my teammate, Elliot Forbes-Robinson. And when this sort of thing happens to you all you can do is just drive the best race you can, never letting up for an instant, hoping the trouble doesn't get any worse in case everybody in front of you runs off the road and lets you win in spite of your difficulties.

LONGER RACES

Until IMSA appeared on the scene with its series of races for GTs and Baby Grand sedans, the only longer races available to the club-type driver were the really long-distance endurance events. IMSA is really filling a need here in my opinion, since longer races are just as interesting and challenging in their own way as a 30-minute sprint. If there's one characteristic that is most important in a longer race, I'd say it was self-discipline. You have to be constantly aware that you've got to make the car last the whole race—keeping the revs at the prescribed limit, being careful to avoid rough pavement on the course, not clipping any corners, staying away from other cars so as to avoid any possible contact and also being alert for cars that are much faster (or much slower) than your own.

There isn't really all that much different in the lap speeds between a longer race and a sprint race. At Daytona, for instance, in the 24-hour race you are only lapping about two to three seconds slower than you would be in a 30-minute sprint. If you could measure it, you'd find that there is hardly any less demanded of the driver in an endurance race but there's a lot less strain on the car. It's a challenge and many drivers who are excellent in sprint races never successfully make the transition to endurance racing because they can't resist going as fast as the car will take them and settle down to the car-saving rhythm that is required.

Driver comfort and good physical condition are naturally even more important in a longer type race than in a 30-minute sprint. Little discomforts that you are barely aware of in a half-hour race may become extremely important when you're out there for a 3-hour driving stint. I've never had any trouble with muscle cramps in a regional or national race, for instance, but in my first 12-hour race, I had lots of trouble with cramps in my hands and in my legs. After this experience I consulted my doctor and he suggested an added intake of calcium in the form of non-fat milk. This has worked for me and I no longer have this trouble.

For a really long race, I've learned I need two or three changes of underwear and driving suits, a couple pairs of gloves, several pairs of socks and even two helmets. The first time I drove in a 24-hour race, this was at Daytona, I also found out that I needed a toothbrush. The drink bottle we used in the car contained a high-sugar content liquid and this left a terrible taste in my mouth that no amount of water, coffee or anything else would get rid of. There is ordinarily not enough time to get any worthwhile amount of sleep between driving stints but if you have soap and water and a fresh towel, plus fresh clothing to get into, you will feel a lot more refreshed when it comes your time to go out again.

There is not as much difficulty in racing at night as you might think before you have actually done it and personally I have never found night racing to be much of a problem. Some drivers don't like to drive during the period when it is getting dark but I have found it to be much the same as it is when you're driving on the highway. The sun may bother you a little when it gets low in the sky and during the period of twilight before it actually gets dark and your lights become more effective, your eyes will be working extra hard, of course.

After it is completely dark, you may even find that it is easier driving at night than in the daytime. When it is dark your headlights only pick out the road and you don't see all those things along the sides of the course that might have been distracting during the daylight hours when you could see them. Depending on the circuit, you may find that you are going just as fast during the night as you were when it was light. At Sebring, because of the complexity of the track, lap times drop maybe two or three seconds at night. But at Daytona, where the course is lighted, there is very little difference in lap speeds between night and day.

In a 6-hour or a 12-hour race you probably will not become tired enough to actually require going to sleep between driving chores. Nevertheless, you should clean up and relax just as much as you can before you have to go out again. In a 24-hour race you do get to the point where you really would like to get some sleep. At times like these it is helpful to have someplace behind the pits where you can at least stretch out and doze. When you get really tired you may sleep like a log and awaken more groggy than you were before you went to sleep and if you're like me, you may doubt that it was the wisest thing to do. It is, though, once you've gotten yourself awake again, as just a couple hours sleep can do you a lot of good.

It is not unheard of for some drivers to take stay-awake pills or one of the stimulant drugs during endurance races. This is an extremely dangerous thing to do because these unquestionably have an adverse effect on your judgment. They may make you feel better temporarily but there is an inevitable period of let-down and you'll soon find that you're in far worse shape than if you hadn't used them at all. This is another example where self-discipline is important. You should be in the best physical shape possible for an endurance race and if you are, you should be able to function at pretty close to maximum efficiency even during a 24-hour race.

It also seems likely to me that the sanctioning organizations are going to become aware that there is a drug problem in racing just as there is outside of racing. And when they do, they're going to impose really tough penalties on drivers found to be using drugs—like a lifetime ban. It's that serious.

But I don't mean to make endurance racing sound more difficult than it is or as if it's so strenuous that the average driver shouldn't leap at the opportunity to participate in an enduro. It's a lot different from club-racing sprints but is a tremendous amount of fun and can be extremely satisfying when it is all over and you've done well.

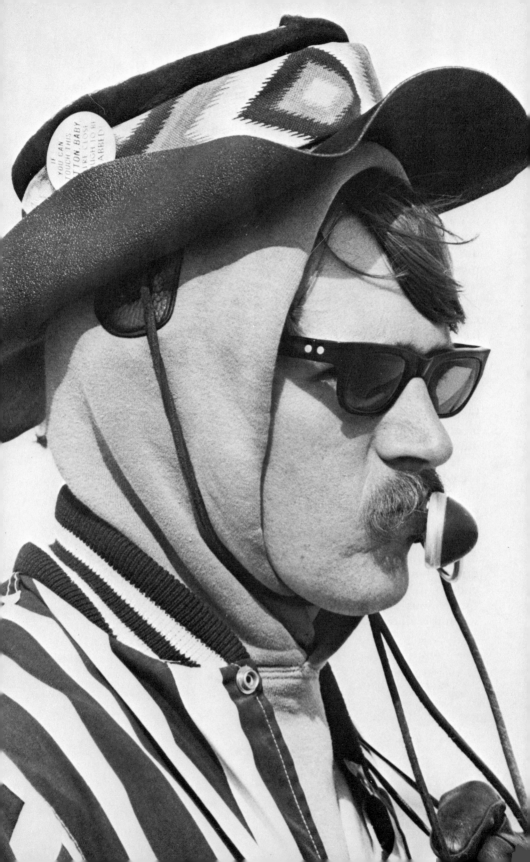

Getting Your License

GETTING A COMPETITION LICENSE in road racing almost always means that you're going to do one of two things—either go through SCCA's driver training program or go to one of the commercial schools that have working agreements with SCCA and IMSA. SCCA is unique in that it is the only large racing organization with a formal driver-training program. IMSA will accept licenses from other major racing organizations or the successful completion of a course at one of the schools they have approved. In most respects, the commercial schools offer more individual attention and a more intensive

109

program. The SCCA philosophy is to start from the beginning, exposing the students to all the preparation and ritual as well as the fundamentals of competition driving. As a result, beginning drivers in SCCA feel that they are a part of the organization much sooner and, having started with a good, broad foundation, may make their mark in racing somewhat more quickly.

Before you appear at your first driver training session you will have already completed the preliminaries. You will have joined SCCA, for instance, and this means that you must belong to the National organization and the local Region as well. From your local Regional Executive or his delegated alternate (Contest Board Chairman, Licensing Program Chairman, or whatever) you get an SCCA physical examination form and undergo a physical. This must be performed by an MD. Your family doctor will usually do. This isn't a stringent examination—they aren't looking for supermen—but it covers enough to make sure that you're in average good health. With the completed medical form, two passport-type photographs and $4 or $5, your Region will issue your SCCA Novice Permit, which is generally called the Novice Logbook. With this you are eligible to begin driver training.

In the logbook there are spaces for you to enter records of your training sessions, the required lecture sessions and for the results of two Regional races to be entered on the satisfactory completion of the driver training program. When you get your Novice Permit, you should also get a copy of the General Competition Regulations (GCR) and the Production Car Specifications but if you've followed my advice, you'll already have these and be thoroughly familiar with them.

When you show up for your first driver training session—and these are traditionally held in the spring at the beginning of the season—everything must be in racing condition. This doesn't mean that your car should be modified to the hilt; that isn't the point. But your car must have the mandatory safety equipment (rollbar, safety harness, scattershield, etc.), tires must be capable of standing up to the speed capability of the car and you must also have all the approved personal safety gear (helmet, fire-resistant suit, gloves, socks and so on).

The basic requirement for completion of the training phase is six hours of satisfactory driving plus the required lecture sessions. In the lecture sessions the main emphasis is on making sure you understand the meaning of the signal flags, why and where they're used and the general rules of the road in competition driving. You may be walked around the circuit, the chief

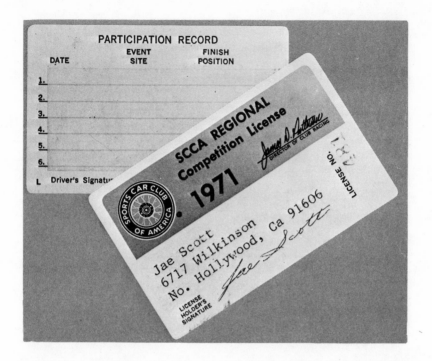

PARTICIPATION RECORD

DATE	EVENT SITE	FINISH POSITION
1.		
2.		
3.		
4.		
5.		
6.		

L   Driver's Signatu~

SCCA REGIONAL
Competition License
1971

SPORTS CAR CLUB OF AMERICA

DIRECTOR OF CLUB RACING

Jae Scott
6717 Wilkinson
No. Hollywood, Ca 91606

LICENSE NO.

LICENSE HOLDER'S SIGNATURE

instructor pointing out the peculiarities of each turn, you may be taken around the course on the back of a truck for the same purpose, and there will probably be a blackboard with a chalk talk given about the proper line for each corner. I am especially in favor of walking around the course with an experienced driver. It is an excellent way to show the inexperienced driver the important things to look for.

After the lecture sessions, you will be assigned to an instructor who will shepherd you through your indoctrination on the course. If you're lucky, the instructor will be a driver you have seen race and he will be familiar with the kind of car you're driving. He will probably first drive you around the course in your car, applying the theory to which you were exposed during the lecture. He will show you the proper line for the turns, caution you about special hazards and other peculiarities that may be encountered on this circuit ("Watch out for the camber change at the exit of this turn..." "Stay wide here, the track is breaking up on the inside..." etc.) and try to instill in you the necessity for driving within your own capabilities.

After that you will be turned loose on the course by yourself to demonstrate how well you've absorbed the knowledge to which you have been exposed. During this time you will be

observed not only by your own instructor but also by other instructors and observers around the circuit. They will try to help you with pointers about where you were off your line and other ways you can improve your driving. Should you push too hard or be so slow that you're a hazard, they'll flag you in and perhaps ask if you're really convinced that you have any business being out there at all.

As a final part of the training program after you've completed everything else you will also participate in short races. These will be run under full racing conditions. You'll be brought down to a rolling start and you'll be free to go just as fast as you can. If you're wise at this point, you'll be careful not to bend any fenders, sail off the circuit, or do anything that will create a doubt in the instructors' minds that you're trying to go faster than your level of skill will permit. As I said, their primary concern at this point is in instilling in you a respect for safety and convincing themselves, before signing off your logbook, that you're a sensible driver and it's safe to turn you loose in a Regional race.

I want to especially emphasize two points. First, your attitude. It is to your benefit to be as receptive as possible during the training period. Your attitude is watched very closely but more important you really do have a great deal to learn at this point. I always listen when a driver I respect is talking about driving and I think most of the better drivers do the same.

Secondly, let me again say that it is extremely important that your car be dependable, ultra-dependable, during this phase of your career. If you have to spend half your time in the pits trying to get your car to run, it will take you twice as long to get through driver training. In some areas, where only a limited number of training sessions are held, this could cause you to miss completing your training phase in one year and you might have to wait until the following season before you could actually start racing.

After successfully completing your training sessions and having your logbook signed off by the chief steward or chief instructor, you will be eligible to participate in Regional races on your Novice Permit. It is important here to *finish* these races as only races that you finish count toward getting your license. DNFs don't count.

When you've completed your two Regional races with your Novice Logbook, you can then apply for an SCCA Regional license, provided you have accomplished the whole novice phase within two calendar years. If you haven't, you start over.

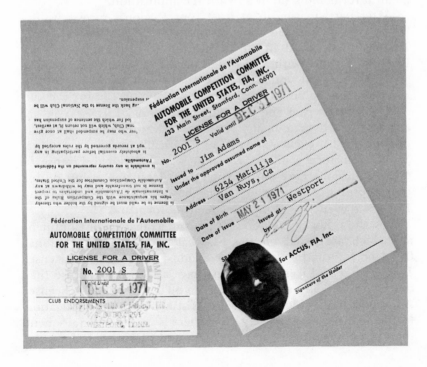

You can continue to run Regional races with your Novice Logbook through the remainder of the year, but only two are required for qualification for your Regional license and additional races run on your Novice Logbook won't be counted for credit. So as soon as you've completed two races, make an application for your Regional license. Until you make application for your Regional license all your paper work is kept by your home Region, probably by the Licensing Chairman.

The Regional License is issued by the SCCA National office and to get it you must send your Novice Permit with the signature of your local Regional Exec (or whoever else is designated for that job), a current medical form (which should be on file in the Regional office) and $5. With the Regional License you are eligible to participate in Regional races and after you have completed four Regionals, with your Regional License, you can then apply for a National License. Again, finishing is important. DNFs don't count. Also, even if you run more than once in a weekend Regional event, you get credit for only one race.

If this extends over more than one season, you will automatically receive an application for renewal of your Regional License. To have it renewed you must have participated in at least two races during the preceding calendar year, submit a new medical form and send in $5 with the application.

After participating in at least four Regional races within a 2-year period, you can apply for your SCCA National License. To get it you send in an application form completed, your Regional License with a record of participation in your Regionals (those run on your Novice Permit don't count), a current medical form (unless you already have one on file for the current calendar year) and $5. With a National License you are eligible to participate in any Regional or National race and some restricted FIA events. You'll automatically receive a renewal application form and to continue your National License in effect you must have participated in at least two events during the preceding year (one of which has to be a National or an FIA-listed event), send in a new medical form and $5.

For the other SCCA series—Can-Am, Trans-Am or Continental—which are listed on the FIA calendar as either National Open or International events, you must have an FIA License. To get an FIA License you must have a National License first but if you do (and send them $10) you will get an FIA license. An application for an FIA license is attached to the application for the SCCA National license and there is no other requirement than to be a National License holder and of course to have the

SCCA DRIVERS SCHOOL

Date: .... Course: ....

Car: .... Class: ....

INSTRUCTOR'S RATING

Judgement			Courtesy	
Technique			Comparative Lap Times	
Attitude				
Reactions				

Rating system 1-5, 1 Lowest, 5 Highest

Total Time Spent on Course:

.... Hours .... Min.

Satisfactory ☐
Not satisfactory ☐

Remarks: ....

....

Signed: ....
            Chief Steward
6

Date: ....

Course: ....

Car: ....

SCCA Region ....

....

Finishing Position O.A. ....

Finishing Position in Class: ......

Satisfactory
Not satisfactor

Remarks: ....

....

....

....

....

Signed: ....
         Ch. Steward, or his des
May be waived
License Chairr

SPORTS CAR CLUB OF AMERICA

NOVICE PERMIT
AND
LOG BOOK

1971

additional ten bucks.

There can be some exceptions to all the above. If you have prior racing experience (either with another club or previously held in SCCA license), then you may not have to go through every phase of the whole program on your way to get a National License. Successful completion of the better private driver training schools (such as Jim Russell's school or the Bob Bondurant school) will also be taken into account and you may be allowed to skip some of the novice phase.

But for most drivers, the simplest and least expensive way is to go through the SCCA program. If you live in a busy racing area (or can afford to travel to races further away) it is possible to go through the Novice and Regional License phases in one season and start your second season as a National License holder. But for most of us, it takes a little longer than that. In my first year I went to two driver training sessions and raced three times (one was a DNF). In my second year I did get enough races completed to qualify for my National License.

By the way, in my first driver training session Richie Ginther was the chief instructor and Ronnie Bucknum was my instructor. You'll find a great many of the better drivers have at some time participated in training as an instructor. After getting my National License I became involved in driver training and I still am. It's a great way to continue your own learning.

When it's time for practice, try to be the first car in line.

Early Races

RIDICULOUS AS IT MAY SOUND, when you are ready to enter your first real race after the completion of your training sessions, one of the problems you may face is getting an entry blank for the race you want to enter. If it's a local race staged by your own Region, you should get one automatically, either in a special mailing or in the pages of the club's local bulletin. But if you don't, call the Regional Executive and ask where you can get one. If the race is being staged by another Region, you will have to go to more effort to get an entry blank by writing or calling the Regional Executive in that Region and asking for one to be sent to you. Getting an entry blank for an IMSA race or one of the smaller independent club races is simpler because only one office is involved. If you're a member, you should get all entry blanks automatically.

Send the entry blank in early and be sure to include your check (they'd rather have a money order—it's surprising how many checks for entry fees bounce). Fill out the entry blank carefully, and though there is a space for you to request the number you'd like to have, don't expect to get it. Competition numbers are generally assigned to established drivers first and as a novice, you'll get what's left. This really doesn't matter. There was a time when I thought I had a lucky number but later discovered that any number is a lucky number if you're a winner with it. If you plan to cut your number out of white or black contact paper instead of painting it on, you'll be much better off if you have to make a change.

The entry fee will range from about $20 to $55 depending on whether it's a Regional or National and whether it's a one-day or a 2-day event. A Regional is generally cheaper than a National (because of the surcharge that goes to the travel fund for the American Road Race of Champions) and the fee varies depending on whether it's a spectator or non-spectator event. Insurance is considerably cheaper for a non-spectator event and usually, but not always, this is reflected in the entry fee.

In some Regions you will receive an acknowledgment of your entry and some Regions even send you your car number with the notice of your acceptance. Either in the acknowledgment letter or on the entry blank there is usually a schedule of events that tells you what's supposed to happen when. Some Regions hold a pre-race technical inspection in the city near which the race is held and whenever this is done, you should make every effort to take the early tech. This is especially important during your first races so you will have time following tech to correct anything the inspection crews may find that doesn't suit them.

Another benefit in taking early tech is that once your car has been inspected and passed, you will be able to pick up your passes for the event and avoid the long lines and delays that are inevitable when you have to go through the routine at the circuit on the day of the event. If you do have to go through tech at the track on the day of the race, it always takes much longer than you anticipate and could prevent you from getting all possible practice in on Saturday morning if you don't allow plenty of time. So if you do have to take tech at the track the day of the event, Get There Very Early.

Usually one of the first things on the schedule is the drivers' meeting on Saturday morning. The officials that will address the group usually include the Chief Steward (he'll emphasize the necessity for safety), the Starter (who'll show you the flags and emphasize the necessity for safety) and whoever else the officials feel is necessary (to emphasize the necessity for safety). But there may be some local ground rules that you'll want to know about—such as warnings about hazardous spots on this particular circuit—so it's always wise to be on hand for the drivers' meetings. About nine out of ten drivers' meetings are unnecessary but once in a while there is some useful information offered that makes you glad you went—changes in scheduling, for instance, so your practice is going to be at 10:00 instead of 2:00 or that your race will now be the first on the program instead of the last. So don't miss a drivers' meeting. It can be important.

When your car arrives at the circuit, you should have nothing left to do except routine pre-race checks such as tire pressures, oil level, etc., and making sure nothing is left in the cockpit that can get loose and roll around. I recommend taking your own fuel to the circuit so you know what kind of fuel you have and so you don't have to wait in line at the gas truck and take a chance on missing part of practice. If your car isn't ready to race when you leave home, you should leave it home.

When the time comes for your class to go out for practice, try to be the first one in line. Get out on the circuit just as early as possible and get just as much practice as you can. In this way you won't have so much traffic to contend with and you can concentrate on learning the course. Also, if anything does go wrong, you may have time to go into the pits for an adjustment, or a change in tire pressures, and still try out the change before the session is over. There's nothing more frustrating than getting out late, discovering there is something that needs changing, coming in to have it changed and then find that your class's time has run out and you can't get back out on the circuit to see if the change corrected the fault or made it worse. So be ready early and make your adjustments early if adjustments must be made.

SATURDAY PRACTICE

Once you are out on the circuit, follow the basic procedures for learning the circuit. You will have already studied the course diagram, hopefully you will have been around it either on the track or on the periphery and you will have made notes about the Type I turns you're going to want to work on first. Also remember the basic fact that it's the smart driver who knows where it isn't important to go fast.

When I'm out on a new circuit for the first time, I have made a guideline that says, "Always use a higher gear than you think you're going to need in a turn." This will help prevent you from overrevving on a corner that surprises you and maybe keep you from doing something embarrassing. There's not much that can make you feel more foolish than bending a valve or spinning a bearing because you thought it looked like a third-gear corner when it was a fourth-gear corner.

During your first several laps of practice, it won't be necessary for your crew to give you lap times. When you've settled down, give them the signal to start passing your lap times on to you and it may be beneficial for them to give you a lap time on each lap. A system I have found to be helpful is for the crew to take your lap time on the back section of the course whenever possible so they can give you your current lap time when you come past the pits. This gives you a better idea of how you're doing and you don't have to try to remember back to the lap before last and think whether that ties in with anything. Timing before the pits also makes it possible for your crew to get you timed on one additional lap in the practice session.

In addition to learning the circuit during practice, you should also be making mental notes about the car. Note the maximum revs you're pulling down the longest straight, the oil pressure at a particular rpm, the water or oil temperature. Also make a note how the brakes are working and if there is a pull in either direction. Are the tires all in balance? Is there anything about the handling or the performance that should be taken care of after practice? Make a strong mental note of all these things because these are things that can easily be forgotten when the car ahead of you spins on the turn before the pits—or when you yourself spin out.

After practice has been completed you should sit down immediately and make notes about the car—how it performed and what needs to be done, if anything—and also to go over in your mind what you learned about driving this circuit and the particular areas you still need to work on. If it's possible later in the day, go to those corners where you weren't perfect and watch other drivers at work on them. See if they know something you didn't find out when you were driving them.

120   You'll normally get only one practice session on Saturday

Mixed-class practice means that you need to be extra careful.

before your race or qualifying session. On Sunday morning there is likely to be only a very short practice and warm-up session. So again, it is essential that you get out early and be ready to go well ahead of time.

It is my recommendation that you do not worry about your competition during your practice session. In fact, it would probably be best for you to stay as clear of your competition as possible so you can learn the course at your own rate of speed and in your own way. If you get into a duel with another driver during practice, you're very likely wasting your time. On the other hand, your crew should be getting lap times on the other drivers in your class who are running times close to your own so they will be able to tell you how you stand after the session is over.

The supplementary regulations for the event may require that your crew take your lap times and that these be turned in for qualifying times. It is essential that you turn in your times immediately, otherwise the people making up the grid sheets may leave you off. Your placement on the grid is very, very important. Don't let yourself be placed on the back of the grid if you don't belong there. And don't turn in a better time than you actually made; it won't do you any good to be placed ahead of faster cars or behind ones that are slower. Your best opportunity for having a good race and learning more about competition will come from being close to those cars that are approximately your own speed.

It has been my habit to eat very lightly at races. This may be partly because it's usually hot at the time of the year that most races are run but the fact that you're usually good and nervous before a race also has something to do with it. It's always wise to have plenty of water with you to drink and when it is very hot either take salt tablets or drink one of the chemical concoctions like Gatorade or Hustle.

As the time for your race approaches, you'll find yourself becoming very nervous and there isn't much you can do about this. Initially you may find that you dislike this period intensely and may even question whether what you're planning to do is really worth all the anxiety. It's important that you maintain your balance, though, because almost everybody will be just as nervous as you. If the pre-race nerves are really serious, you may even become actively ill and I've known more than one driver who regularly threw up before starting a race. If this happens to you, perhaps you should see a psychiatrist—not to be cured of it but for the concentration tricks he may be able to suggest. One driver I knew got such a trick from a psychiatrist—his solution was to grip a rubber ball in his hand, grip it just as tightly as he could and concentrate on gripping it—and it worked for him though he was admittedly never what you might call relaxed before the race started. But at least he didn't throw up anymore.

THE START

Before the start of your own race it is a good idea to observe the start of a couple other races. In this way you get an idea how this particular starter operates. SCCA and almost all other racing organizations use a rolling start, so you should take note exactly where (relative to the position of the cars in the front row) this particular starter has the habit of dropping the flag. He will usually do this when the cars reach a certain spot on the starting straight. If you decipher his style, you can be ready. You should drop back a little bit just before the lead cars get to that point. In this way you can be moving up a little faster than the other cars when the flag actually drops.

It's very important in the ordinary sprint-type race to get a good start and to take every possible advantage to improve your position in the early part of the race. The chances of picking up a couple spots—or a couple other drivers picking you off—are excellent in the first couple of turns. Of course this has to be done very carefully as the cars will be running close together at this stage of the race and you also need to be alert to what's going on in front of you in case somebody loses it. The best

In many regions, weighing the cars keeps everybody honest.

general rule is to stay to the inside so you can't be squeezed out and have the whole line go under you. But if you know your competition, there are also times when you can stay outside, brake later and still get into line ahead of another driver.

Your nervousness will all be gone by this time and you can settle down and concentrate on driving your race.

As the race goes on, you'll find that your rear view mirror can be either a help or a hindrance. It can be a definite disadvantage if you begin watching it to the point where you're so worried by the car behind that you begin to make mistakes through loss of concentration. This has happened to me. I remember a Saturday race in 1963 at Dodger Stadium when a friend of mine was right on my tail and it bothered me so much that I was bobbling in the turns and eventually let him get past and win the race. On Sunday I was so determined to win that I began the race by turning my mirror down so I couldn't see anything in it. I went off the grid just as hard as I could, got the lead, concentrated on what I was doing and drove as fast as possible. About halfway through the race I readjusted my mirror to get an idea how I was doing and I was so far ahead that I couldn't even see anyone behind me.

In your first few races, use the race as an opportunity to practice. Improve your line on the all-important Type I turns and constantly strive to do it better every time around even though you know your position in the race is secure. Develop mental discipline so that you are concentrating throughout the entire race. You don't need to take chances to do this but keep your mind on what you're doing no matter how hopelessly far

123

behind you are and even if you know you're not going to catch anybody. A race is the best kind of practice there is.

PIT STOP

The usual SCCA Regional or National is so short that a pit stop during the race precludes your doing well for position either overall or in class. But until you get your National License, it's important that you rejoin the race if you can and be running when the flag falls.

Your pit crew should have all their basic tools with them and ready for use at all times in case you do have to come in during the race. A jack, lug wrench and a spare tire (don't forget to have the right pressure in it) should be ready and at least a set of pliers, screwdriver, safety wire and a roll of racer's tape.

If you have to stop and add gas or oil during a sprint race, you did something wrong. Before the race be sure that you're going to have at least as much gas as you'll need for the event—plus a couple gallons extra. It's cheap insurance.

Pit stops for longer races should be carefully planned and regularly practiced. It's a good idea to study the techniques at a USAC or NASCAR race and then organize your pit stops so your crew can work with that same kind of efficiency.

AFTER THE RACE

At the completion of the event be sure that you've made mental notes of the basic functioning of the car—max revs on the longest straight, oil temp (or water temp) and oil pressure. These go into your race notebook, along with all other pertinent information you may want or need later. Also be sure to write down anything you noticed during the race that wasn't functioning perfectly—maybe the clutch was hanging up occasionally, or your brakes began to pull in the last few laps, or your tires began to lose their bite after they got good and warm so maybe you should raise (or lower) the pressures in the future.

After getting home from the race, I highly recommend that you go to work immediately to get the car ready for the next race. That's the time to look at everything that was suspect the last time, not the night before the next race. You probably won't have the manpower to do a complete teardown and rebuild between races but until you know your car thoroughly (again, record everything you do in your notebook), you should be doing a lot of extra work checking the bearings for wear, doing a compression check, adjusting the valves, examining the points, keeping an eye on the water pump drive belt, checking the clutch free-play, measuring the amount of brake pad wear and so on.

There's a product called Gunk that is one of the best friends the car-preparation crew ever had. It's a water-soluble solvent that you either spray or brush on and then wash off with water. When you've finished making greasy fingerprints in the engine compartment, go over it with Gunk or something similar and clean everything until it sparkles. Not only is this good sense from a preparation point of view, it also has a marvelous psychological effect on the tech inspection crew before the next race. When you open your hood and they shine their flashlights in, if they smell the distinctive odor of fresh Gunk and see a sparkling clean engine compartment, they're predisposed to think that here's a guy who knows how to prepare a car. Having everything nice and clean also gives you a far better chance to spot any leaks or seepage so that you will catch such things before getting to tech.

After you've been racing for a while, you'll begin to know how often you can expect to have to replace various components. When I was racing my Porsche Speedster, I checked the main and rod bearing wear after every race by looking in the oil filter for particles of metal and routinely replaced them every third race. I did this because I'd checked them time and again and found that, consistently, they were beginning to show signs of wear after three races. So I didn't take a chance. I changed them early. Bearings are lots cheaper than crankshafts. I also found it to be a good idea to re-check valve clearances not only before every race weekend but also after a Saturday race and before a Sunday race. Points clearance is another item for regular pre-race checking. And with a highly tuned engine, I think fresh plugs are wise nearly every race.

Also, if you make any engine modifications between races— or alter the suspension—it is a good idea to try them out before going to the next race. Admittedly this is difficult to do if your car isn't licensed to drive on the street. For a pure power item, you can sometimes use a local dragstrip and learn something about the car's acceleration (if you've been there before and have recorded your elapsed time and trap speed) in that way. Admittedly, though, there's nothing like having a circuit available for test driving after you've made modifications and we'll talk about that next.

Testing & Development

EVEN IN CLUB RACING, a well organized testing and development program very often spells the difference between being a winner and an also-ran. The private entrant's budget will not often extend far enough to cover a major development program but the more testing he does, the better the driver he is going to be and the better the car is going to be.

For the driver, testing gives him a chance to continuously drive the car at racing speeds free of worry about other competitors on the circuit and without the anxieties that are always present during a brief pre-race practice session. As in any athletic endeavor, the more you practice, the more you learn and the better you become at the sport. For the car, a test session is the place to try out new combinations and do chassis tuning.

ENGINE TESTING

Engine improvements, ideally, should be tested on an engine dynamometer. Or, in the case of moderately powerful production cars, a chassis dyno can be used to good effect. Chassis dynos are much more widely available than they were a few years ago since many auto dealers now have installed them in their diagnostic centers. On a chassis dyno you simply drive the car onto the rollers and then, after the instrumentation is hooked up, you go up through the gears until you're in the rpm range you want to use. You put your tachometer on, say 6000 rpm, and read directly from the power output dial on the dyno. If you have tested your car on the same dyno and under approximately the same conditions of temperature and humidity so you have a base line, you can then see exactly what effect your modifications have had. The actual figures are not in themselves as important as the increase that has been realized.

With regular sessions on a chassis dyno, you can keep tabs on how you're doing. A good many production car drivers use the chassis dyno for final race tuning to adjust their jetting, ignition settings, etc., in order to avoid the possibility of getting to the track and then finding out they're not getting everything the car is capable of.

If you don't have a local garage which will let you use their chassis dyno after hours and give you a friendly price, it can be pretty costly, of course. Chassis dyno time is reasonably expensive on the open market, on the order of $10 minimum and up to about $30 per hour. But if your racing budget will stretch to cover it, the benefits are undoubtedly worth it.

An engine dyno is an even more specialized piece of equipment. Ordinarily you should use an engine dyno when you are making major engine modifications or want to experiment with a number of different components to find out exactly what effect they have. If, for instance, there are three different kinds of pistons available for your engine, you may want to try all three to see which works best for you. When you're doing something like this, it is obviously much easier when you have the engine out of the car. An engine dyno is usually more completely instrumented than a chassis dyno and this makes it possible to make a more thorough analysis of the modifications.

With an engine dyno, the horsepower at the flywheel is meater to race an established marque. If you have a car whose manufacturer couldn't care less whether you race it or not, all the development costs fall on the individual and this makes it awfully expensive in most cars.

HANDLING

To test the handling of your car and the effect that modifications have on the handling, you need a regular place where you can do the evaluation. If you're lucky, there will be a circuit nearby that you can rent for a moderate fee. Or, sometimes, three or four drivers can get together and rent a circuit for a day or an afternoon. If you can do this, you will avoid the risks inherent in trying to test on some quiet back road, which is never very satisfactory since you know you're going to have to make your session very brief if you're to avoid the attention of the local constabulary.

I have found it best, when test driving, to establish a test driving speed and stick to it. For testing, I go just a little slower than my absolute maximum. In this way, I can be more consistent and this is the most important factor in test driving. In other words, in the equation you are testing, the driver should be a constant. He should drive exactly the same way every lap so the changes that have been made to the car will account for changes in speed, not because the driver is trying harder or using more revs. By driving just a little less than the maximum, the driver can also concentrate more on what the car is doing and try to analyze the problems.

During the development program we carried out on the Porsche 914/6 at Willow Springs, we learned many things. One of the problems we had with the car early in the program was that it was breaking loose rather early on the highspeed right-hand sweeper. This is a turn where, if the car is working just right, you can go around very nearly flat out in top gear. But with the 914/6, I could feel that it wanted to oversteer in this corner so the rear end would come out abruptly. We worked and worked on this problem. I'd go out, drive the course as consistently as I could, really concentrating on what was happening. Then I'd stop at the pits and try to tell my team manager, Richie Ginther, what the car was doing. He could deduce from what I said that the cause had to be some place in the rear suspension. So we tried different shock settings, changed rollbars, tire pressures and everything, just about, that we could think of. After each change I'd go out and try it again. The lap speeds varied a little with the changes but the same problem of

sured and the operator will generally use a set of cor[
factors to come up with "standard conditions" horse[
With an engine dyno you can also plot horsepower and [
curves and be accurate with them where, with a chassis [
the slippage between the rollers and the tires tends to n[
full curve of power vs. rpm figures somewhat suspect.

To sum it up, an engine dyno is used for major chang[
development work while a chassis dyno is simpler fo[
tuning and checking out minor changes that don't requ[
moval of the engine.

A complete engine development program is tremen[
expensive, and almost no independent driver has the ki[
financing that is required for such a program. Fortunate[
you, the major distributors in production category raci[
this kind of work for their own teams and then make the r[
of their programs available to independents driving the [
kinds of cars. This may take the form of a competition t[
manual that gives you chapter and verse on how to [
yourself, or the factory-backed development team may be [
to sell you everything you need from a set of special rod [
or pistons to a completely prepared, dyno-tuned, race-r[
engine. There are also independent engine builders who d[
same thing for those classes where the factories don't have[
direct involvement. All these highly specialized firms are [
prime sources for information and if you have a problem [
can't solve, they are very often able to help.

This isn't to say that it isn't possible to develop a par[
your own. Through the years I've figured out a number of v[
to improve on the original factory design and in a couple [
I've gone to the expense of having castings made or sp[
machine work done to get exactly what I want in the way [
piston design or a camshaft. It is expensive, though, and [
really have to be serious for it to be worthwhile.

All of the manufacturers who have a competition progr[
are as helpful as they can afford to be in club racing. It's g[
business for them. The more cars of their make that are be[
raced, the better it is for them. And if you become known a [
serious competitor who is attracting favorable attention to t[
marque, you will probably find that you can get special comp[
tition parts at a considerable discount over the regular ret[
price. It's no secret that some distributors will help out a b[
ter-than-average competitor who needs it even though he isn[
associated with the regular factory team.

Because development is so expensive, it is almost always be[

You not only have to beat the drivers, you also have to beat team managers like Pete Brock, Kas Kastner and Richie Ginther.

abrupt oversteer was still there.

What we finally discovered was that the left rear shock absorber was bottoming out. As the car went into the sweeper, the car would lean over and come up against the stop. In other words, all the suspension travel was used up and when this point was reached the tires couldn't hold on any more and the rear end would start to come around. We cured this by removing a stop at the end of the shock travel—it couldn't have been more than three-quarters of an inch of difference—and that cured it. The car felt so much better after the stop was removed that I then had trouble holding it down to our testing speed. With that change alone we picked up more than a second a lap even when I didn't drive any harder or take any more out of the car.

This kind of development testing is the sort of thing you never have time to do during a pre-race practice session. And pre-race practice isn't the time or place to be doing such things anyway. When you're at the course getting ready for a race, the car should be the constant and the driver, who is learning the turns and studying the course is the variable.

It is axiomatic in all testing that you should never try more than one change at a time. I've seen any number of drivers get themselves completely screwed up by making too many changes all at once and then never be able to sort out which was helping him to go faster and which was slowing him down. Even the pros do this sometimes. It happens at Indianapolis every year. A team will start out, go at a pretty good speed and then begin changing things. A week later they may be going slower than they did when they started. I remember a story I heard about

Dan Gurney once when he went to Daytona to drive a Ford for the Holman-Moody team. The mechanics set the car up before Dan arrived and as soon as he drove it, he wanted everything changed. So they grumbled to themselves, made the changes that Dan requested and, sure enough, he went slower. This went on all through the week until, finally, the day before the race, they were right back to the same settings they'd started with. Incidentally, I think that was the last race Dan drove for Holman-Moody. In stock car racing they have a saying that goes: Drivers are like light bulbs. You screw one in and if he doesn't light up, you screw in another one.

So don't outsmart yourself by trying to do more than one thing at a time.

TIRE TESTING

Tire testing is another important part of any development program because you have to find out what works best for the car you're using. In tire testing, it is important to have the car and the driver as the constants so that the tires themselves will be the only variables. If you are a private entrant, you probably won't have the tire companies after you to drive test sessions for them and help them with their development program. Nevertheless, you can do a limited amount of such testing for yourself. You can experiment with pressures and you can also compare one brand, or one compound, against another.

The quickest way to determine optimum tire pressures is on a skid pad. Unfortunately these aren't very often available to individual drivers and I wish that every circuit that's built would include one in their plans. With about a 200-ft radius, you can very quickly arrive at the pressures that work best for your car with that particular tire. You start out with the pressures on the low side, warm up the tires with a lap or two, then time three or four consecutive laps to get a good average. Then, by increasing pressures in, say, two psi increments, you can continue this until you have achieved your maximum cornering speed.

A pyrometer is also a worthwhile instrument to have when you're testing tires. You've probably seen the Goodyear and Firestone tire technicians taking tire temperatures at some of the big races. They aren't just checking to see if the tires are running too hot. They're recording information that can be of direct help to the driver. To some drivers, the information these technicians pass on seems like black magic. "You're getting a little too much understeer. Maybe you ought to try a little more pressure in the fronts." Or, "The rear end is breaking loose, you might decamber the rear wheels about half a degree."

What they're doing, of course, is interpreting what the tire temperatures are telling them and then translating this into information the driver can use. If the front tires are running too much hotter than the rears, then the front tires have been scrubbing more than the rears and that means understeer. If the inside shoulder of the rear tire is hotter than the outside shoulder, then there's too much negative camber and that should be changed. For absolute maximum adhesion, the tire should be absolutely flat across the face of the tread in a turn and when this is true, the temperature across the tread should be even. If you have too much pressure, the center of the tread will run hotter than the shoulders. Of course the temperature of the fronts and rears will be slightly different since almost no car is absolutely neutral-steering but there's a range that your car should stay inside.

If you don't have a pyrometer, you can sometimes learn a great deal simply by placing your palm across the tread as soon as the car comes into the pits from a hot lap. You can get a hint about tire pressures in this way (the tread should be the same temperature all the way across the tread) and if your suspension is adjustable, you can sometimes make changes that will improve adhesion. Most cars come from the factory with the suspension set at a compromise position that is best for running with a full load. For racing, especially if the car is lighter than it was when it came from the factory, the suspension will need to be readjusted to remove some of the camber from the wheels so the tires sit absolutely square with the ground.

Again, these are things that need to be done in the testing session, not the day of the race. When you get to the track you may want to check just to be sure you're right on, but don't start a development program on a race weekend.

INFORMAL TESTING

Informal testing is what I call those times when you can't get to a chassis dyno to check out a change or can't get to a racing circuit to test a change you've made in the handling. Informal testing has to be done on the road and while this is far from ideal, it's probably better than nothing.

If you're going to be doing this you need at least two different kinds of road. You need a flat level stretch where you can compare acceleration figures before and after your modifications and you need at least one good constant-radius turn. On the flat and level stretch you can take a passenger with a stop

*Careful work and
fine detailing on
C Production engines:
Triumph TR6,
Porsche 914/6
and Datsun 240Z*

watch and, being careful to shift at exactly the same rpm every time, measure how long it takes you to get from max revs in, say, second gear to max revs in third. Your passenger, who should be operating a hundredths-reading stop watch, clicks the watch on the 2-3 shift and then again on the 3-4 shift. If your modifications to the engine have had any effect, they will be discernible in the acceleration of the car. And by using an intermediate gear, you don't have to shatter all the speed limits in your corner of the state. Of course it is important to use this same stretch of road for all such tests as your eye won't tell you for sure whether it is absolutely level or exactly the same gradient as another that looks equally level.

The constant-radius turn that is suitable for evaluation handling will be harder to find. For this you will probably need to station an observer at a point where he can see that no one else is coming and also where he can click his watch at pre-determined points before and after the turn to measure your speed through that corner. If it's a fairly flat turn, you can probably run it in both directions, which will also tell you something if you keep records of all this in your notebook.

You have to also remember that this sort of testing can be dangerous as well as being illegal. I think all states have traffic regulations that forbid using public streets and highways for doing performance testing of automobiles and you can therefore have a ticket hung on you even though you weren't actually exceeding the posted speed limits.

Handling checks made in this manner will only get you in the ball game, not allow you to make your adjustments exact. So don't try to go too far with this kind of testing and don't expect to learn much till you can get on a real race course.

All this talk about testing may seem like it's a bit excessive for being competitive in club racing where it's all supposed to be fun. But I'm afraid that such programs as these are pretty nearly essential if you're going to have a chance of winning as tough as the competition is these days. And even if the driver you're up against isn't a pro, his team manager may be—and you'll have to beat him too.

Winning

ULTIMATELY, WINNING is what racing is all about and when this begins to happen to you, a number of things will begin to change. For one thing, racing will become easier for you. You'll go into the races with fewer anxieties because you'll have confidence in your car and you'll have fewer doubts about your own abilities. You will also find that there is a change in other people's attitude toward you. When you first begin to do well, everybody becomes your friend and you'll suddenly have friends you never even knew about. Pretty girls who ignored you in the past may find you worth being nice to—though I confess I haven't had a lot of trouble in this regard. Less successful drivers will seek your opinion on how to drive a certain corner and how to set their cars up like yours. A newspaper or a magazine may do a story about you. This is all pretty flattering and you would have to be something less than normal not to be affected by it.

SPONSORSHIP

Getting a sponsor is what nearly every driver in racing wants. All the way from the Formula Vee owner who is just starting out to the established Can-Am pro, drivers are looking for sponsors. Sponsors are rare and elusive animals, hard to find and even harder to keep. Some drivers seem to have a magical quality for finding somebody else to foot the bills. And other drivers, even though they're just as good, never have any luck with sponsors at all.

There are good sponsors in racing and there are bad sponsors. The good ones, I'd say, are probably the little ones, a dealer or a garage owner who doesn't put a lot of money into the project but will come up with parts, or let you use his facilities for development work and maybe come up with the money for a couple of tires when you're right down to your last buck and you've got your back against the wall. This kind of sponsor knows what racing is all about and doesn't expect a miracle every Sunday afternoon. It's usually good business for a small dealer or shop owner because it attracts other customers to his shop and even though race preparation isn't his specialty (there's no money to be made in race preparation, everybody knows that), success in club racing does have a beneficial rub-off with knowledgeable spectators.

Personally, over the long haul I'd rather have one good sponsor like this than one of those at the other extreme who doesn't know anything about racing but gets all excited about it, temporarily. This type has the money to do it right, he lets you help him spend it to get a first-class car, you travel first class and you think, boy, now I've got it made. This type goes all out, for a while, but he's likely to be fickle and while road racing may be his big thing today, tomorrow he could just as easily get hooked on airplanes, boats, tiddlywinks or girls with big bazooms. By the middle of the season you could be wondering where your next set of spark plugs is coming from.

Getting a sponsor of any kind will probably only be possible after you've demonstrated at least some degree of accomplishment. Probably only after winning races. And in a class that is receiving attention in the pre-race publicity and the post-race reports. If you're driving a D sports racing car—and I don't mean to demean that class, it's great for the guys who are in it—it is very unlikely that anything like real sponsorship will ever come about.

In club racing, the distributors or dealers of the cars being raced are probably your best source of help. Several of the manufacturers have set up performance bonus programs for drivers racing their cars and these are available to private owners. The amounts these companies pay vary with the company and with the kind of race. You might get as much as $500 for winning a National in a popular class and maybe as little as $50 (or nothing) for a class win in a Regional. To qualify for these performance bonuses, it's up to you to send them evidence of your performance (a copy of the results, for instance) and some manufacturers require that you register with them as a part of the program in order to be eligible. The SCCA National office keeps in close touch with all the manufacturers about such things and will furnish you with the appropriate names and addresses to contact.

Don't expect to get any free tires from the tire companies. Tire company support comes only to those drivers who are involved in major racing events that they can use in their advertising. Free spark plugs are sometimes available but this depends on the event and you'd better have your own supply along. If you carry the right decal, you can sometimes get free oil. About the only product you can depend on being furnished to you free is STP, which consistently spends more money in racing than any other company in the country. STP will also sometimes offer contingency money, even for club races, provided you carry one of their decals on your car.

I've gone pretty much the whole route so far as sponsorship is concerned. I started out paying for my own car and paying list price for everything. In my early races, I carried the name of a local service station on the side in exchange for being allowed to use their facilities for some of the work I couldn't do in my garage at home. It didn't cost them a nickel and I doubt if they ever got a nickel's worth of business because of me. It was about three years before I had a sponsor that did me any real good—or for whom my racing did much good either. This was Roger Bursch, the manufacturer of Bursch Exhaust Systems and owner of a garage in Pasadena. I know that Roger's help was important to me and I also believe that my success in racing was equally good for his business. I used a Bursch Exhaust System on my car and because my car was fast, pretty soon almost everybody that was racing a Porsche had one too—plus several hundred other Porsche and VW drivers who weren't racing but wanted them for use on the street. The success we had in racing also brought people into Roger's shop for service; even though they didn't want their cars put into competition tune, the dependability of my car helped convince them that Roger's shop did good work. This was pretty nearly an ideal arrangement for an independent driver and Roger and I stayed together for five years. The arrangement I had with Roger was completely informal; sometimes I would pay wholesale price for parts I needed, sometimes he'd give them to me without charge. Sometimes I'd pay for a set of tires, sometimes he would, depending on the state of our individual finances at the time. We did a couple of development programs on camshafts and pistons, working with local manufacturers to get something that would work better than anything else available, and on those we shared the costs with the understanding that I'd have the benefit of the parts and he could sell the same parts to other competitors who wanted them. Nevertheless, it was still nothing like full sponsorship and once I found I was capable of winning races, the cost of racing grew and grew. If you're running at the back of the pack, you can afford to run something less than the best and stickiest tires. But when you're running at the front, you have to spend the money to stay there.

One of the turning points in my own career came in 1964 when I made up my mind to do everything that was necessary to win everything in sight. No matter what the car needed, I'd put it on; the latest, stickiest tires (even though they lasted only one race), a new clutch before every race, special pistons, a new camshaft, and whatever else it took. It put a real strain on the family finances that year but it paid off for me and I was able to win 11 races and also win the National Championship that year in E Production. If I had tried to cut corners anyplace, I doubt if the same results could have been achieved.

It wasn't until 1968—my eighth year in the sport—that I became fully sponsored, driving somebody else's car, having somebody else responsible for preparing the car and towing it to the race, having all my travel expenses paid and getting performance bonus money in addition. At that point I think I had it as good as any driver in club racing. But it was still an avocation with me, not a business, and I sure couldn't live on what I made from racing. I'm not complaining, you understand, I'm simply trying to explain that no matter how well you do in club racing, it isn't a sport at which you can make a living, no matter how successful you are.

There are, of course, a number of people who do make a living from their activities associated with club racing. Those who come to mind first are the factory team managers and mechanics. There are also a few highly skilled driver-mechanics who are able to support their own racing by preparing cars for other people. But even among the best known club racing teams in the country I don't think there's a single one that has a fulltime professional driver who makes his living just from being a racer. There just isn't that kind of money in it. If you want to make your living being a competition driver, you have to be a professional—and that's pretty much a whole new ball game.

Going Pro

BECOMING A PROFESSIONAL DRIVER is a state to which many drivers aspire but which very few *ever* achieve. In this country right now there are probably fewer than a hundred (yes, that's what I said, 100) drivers who are making a decent living—or a living of any kind—as professional drivers. And a lot fewer than 25 who are making money in any really worthwhile amounts. Mario Andretti is reported to have made $900,000 a couple years ago but I'd be willing to bet that for every professional driver who makes as

much as $50,000 a year from racing, there are 50 who make less than $15,000.

This isn't to say it can't be done. Let's take the example of George Follmer. George first got into competition by driving his own Volkswagen in Southern California slaloms. Later he bought himself a Porsche Speedster, went through the Cal Club's driver training program in 1960 and went on to become one of the best club drivers in the area. He ran himself out of money several times, became inactive while he built up his cash reserves again and in 1965 bought himself a Lotus 23-Porsche. He campaigned it in the U.S. Road Racing Championship and won the championship that year. Through this he was able to get the opportunity to race professionally for somebody else but it is important to remember that up until this time he had bought his own cars, prepared them himself, and bore all his own expenses. In his career he has gone from slaloms in a Volkswagen to a factory ride in a Mustang Trans-Am sedan, then to USAC championship cars, the Can-Am championship and Formula 1. So it can be done. But don't forget that George spent his own money for a good long time and even now I seriously doubt that he's getting as rich as he could have become if he'd stayed in the insurance business.

Mark Donohue is an equally good example. Mark started out in SCCA club racing on the East Coast and for several years was car owner, chief mechanic, driver and the sole financial support of his own cars. Walt Hansgen recognized that Mark had the talents required to be a first-class driver and in 1965 told Mark that they were going to co-drive a Ferrari at Sebring. (Mark's reaction to that was, "Do you think I'm ready for it?") After that Mark began to think of himself as a professional driver but it wasn't until he began his association with Roger Penske that he quit his job as an engineer and became a full-time professional. And again—like George—he paid his own money to race his own car for a good long time before he became a successful pro.

If you do go into professional racing you will probably find that you will have to have another job to be sure of paying the rent. In the events themselves, you will be introduced into a much more serious level of competition. The level of car preparation is higher and the level of driving skill is higher. And if you can't keep up, your career as a professional driver is going to be very brief.

THINK IT OVER

First of all, you have to ask yourself if becoming a professional racing driver is what you really want to do. You can be a club racer until you're old and gray and still regard it as a hobby that is independent of whatever it is you do with the rest of your life. But if you are going to be a full-fledged professional driver, you have to make a total commitment to it. You're going to have to give up your regular job or career, assuming you have one. If you're in a business of your own, you're probably not going to have the time to dedicate to it to keep it running smoothly. If you're married, you should be aware that the divorce rate among professional drivers is extraordinarily high, since not many women welcome the kind of constant strain that being a professional driver's wife inevitably entails. There's just no doubt about it, it takes a special kind of dedication (or obsession) to become a professional driver and such a decision should not be taken lightly. I've known too many drivers who've gotten serious about going pro and have made the necessary sacrifices in their lives only to wind up either never quite getting a ride that was good enough or not having quite enough ability. Believe me, there's nothing sadder than a person who has taken a hunk of years out of his life to chase a will-o'-the-wisp that always eludes him. I don't personally have that kind of dedication and I know it. I've done some professional racing but I've never let myself fall into the trap of believing it would be worth giving up my business career and personal life on the chance that I might be a success at professional racing.

But for the sake of discussion, let's say you've made the decision and that you're going to take the step into full-time professional racing. We're not going to get into all those aspects of a professional racing program that involve selecting a car, preparing it, and entering it, or all the logistics involved in the operation of a racing team. Professional racing is so different from club racing in these respects that it would take another book this size just to lay out all the details. But I do think I can give you some hints that might be helpful.

FIRST THINGS FIRST

When an agreement has been reached for you to drive a car in professional competition, it is essential that the various aspects of the agreement between you and the car owner be set down in writing. It isn't necessary for this to be a full-blown, lawyer-legal document (although some owners insist on this) but it is very important that both you and the owner fully understand and agree on the terms. You'll want several things spelled out, not only such things as the division of prize money and who pays which expenses but also to what extent you participate in sponsorship arrangements, how much of your time is going to be required for public relations or sponsor relations, what insurance coverage is in effect, restrictions on your driving for other car owners or other sponsors, and so on. Professional racing is a highly organized business these days and this is the reason that so many of the bigger names have personal managers to take care of all the business arrangements. You won't need that level of expertise when you first make the step to professional racing but it is always important to do business in a businesslike manner.

If it is possible for you to arrange it, you should also spend some time in the car on a race track without the distractions and emotionally charged atmosphere that exists when the race is three days off and there are still a thousand things yet to be done to get ready for the race. This means that the team should rent a racing circuit where you can drive at your own speed while you become accustomed to the car.

You should be very subjective at this time, learning how this particular car functions and also how you are going to function in it. The first order of business is to make the car suit you better. It seems ridiculous but many of the cars that are built for professional racing don't do a very good job of making it

146

easy for the driver. In other words, a designer may spend hours and hours determining exactly where a suspension pickup point should go but almost completely ignore having the controls logically arranged and properly located so the driver can operate the machine at maximum efficiency. Even the very best racing cars seem to suffer from this, so the better you are able to make the machine accommodate you, the better job you'll be able to do in it.

The seating position is extremely important and should receive your utmost attention. Some cars have only a thin layer of padding over the tub and leave it up to the driver to either live with it or add the essential padding to make it habitable. Or if another driver has been driving this car and has fixed the seat to suit his backside, you may have to pull padding out of one area and add it to another so it suits you. Because of my long legs, I've always found it very difficult to be completely comfortable in the Can-Am cars I've driven. Pieces of tubing that are part of the structure get in the way, or the sharp corner of the tub hits me in the wrong place, and if I didn't build a pad over those places my legs would get sore in those spots and distract me from maximum concentration.

Next in order of importance is the location and accessibility of the controls. Maybe the steering wheel is skinnier than you like, or fatter. The shift lever may be too short or too tall. The relative positions of the brake pedal and accelerator may not be right for you. If there's a fuel tank switchover valve, is it where you can reach it and operate it with a minimum amount of distraction? All these things are important in your being able to drive this car to the best of your ability.

During this first session with the car you should also analyze the vision you have out of the car. Perhaps you need a bit of windscreen trimmed off here, or maybe you're taller than the previous driver and need a little more screen to keep your head from being buffeted by the wind. Even though you're on the track by yourself, you'll also want to check out the rear view mirror. Maybe it isn't in the right location for you. If it's too low, you may not be able to see it without raising your head. Or it could be located where there's too much vibration and a support brace needs to be added.

At the same time you have to become acquainted with the instrumentation. First of all, you have to be able to see the instruments and you should be able to do this without turning your head or moving your eyes more than a few degrees off the road. You also have to learn what the individual dials mean, 147 where the needles should be and get used to reading them at a glance. It's also necessary to store that information in your memory so you can tell the pit crew what they want to know when you return to the pits.

All through this period of getting acquainted with the car, analyze everything about the machine that affects your operation of it. Obviously, you can't expect the crew to completely rebuild the car just to make you happy, but it is worth it to do everything possible to make it better for you. Because the level of competition in professional racing is so high, you cannot afford to overlook *anything* that will improve your chances of doing well.

THE CREW

When you were in club racing, chances are you were the car owner, chief mechanic and head gopher as well as the driver. You set the schedule for things to be done and if you didn't like the way one member of the crew did his job, you replaced him with somebody else or you did it yourself. As a professional driver, you may not have anything at all to say about who works on the car or play any except the most incidental part in its preparation. For this reason it is of great importance that you give special attention to the various personalities that are an inevitable part of every racing team. A crew can make you or break you in professional racing and it seems to me that a lot of drivers never realize this.

By their very nature, racing mechanics are a strange breed. They'll bitch and moan, show up drunk, get in fights, make smart remarks about you under their breath and seemingly do everything they can think of to make your life miserable. But they'll also work straight through for three nights in a row to get you on the starting grid after you did it all wrong in the hairpin, and they'll give your car a kind of blind devotion they wouldn't give to their wives. I think this is because they really understand what racing is all about. They know, far better than a lot of drivers, that a racing team is just that, a team, and if everybody doesn't work for the team they don't have anything.

To the crew, you're just another part of the team and just about the worst thing you can do is treat them like you're more important than they are. You may have been a pretty big shot when you were a club racer but as a professional driver you're just another cog.

There are some car owners and team managers that regard drivers as little more than an essential evil and don't want them to do anything except get in and drive. In all honesty, they have a point. Some drivers get too involved in the preparation of the car when they aren't really qualified to do it. A driver like this can screw up all the work that the best crew in the world can do. I've known drivers who couldn't tell the crew anything more than "it handles funny"; if you're one of those, don't try to snow the crew by trying to tell them how to do their jobs.

So it's absolutely essential that you get to know the crew and that you operate with them as part of the team.

TESTING

After you've gotten settled into the car, then and only then can you settle down to some serious testing. As mentioned earlier, in testing sessions it is most effective to drive just a little bit under the maximum so that you are able to be consistent, lap after lap, and let the changes that have been made in the car change the lap times rather than the amount of effort you are putting in. Communicating with the crew is extremely important at this time so you must concentrate on what you're expected to tell them. It isn't going to be any help to anybody if you come into the pits and confess that you don't know whether it's better or worse.

At the end of the testing session, after everything is done that can be done, you'll want to crank on a few of the fastest laps you can. You do this not only to assess the full potential of the car but also to give the team's morale a little boost. There's nothing more discouraging for a team than to spend a day or a week testing a car and not be able to see any significant improvement as a result of all their labors.

TO THE RACE

A professional driver doesn't ordinarily concern himself with the logistics of getting the car from race to race but he does have to coordinate his own travel with that of the team. When a crew has worked all night to get to the circuit in time for the first practice session only to find that the driver hasn't bothered to get there until later, it's bad for morale. So plan your schedule to fit in with the crew's plans, be there well in advance of the appointed time and be ready to drive the car when they have it ready for you.

Just as when you were racing your own car in club events, there are many details that you will have to take care of on your own. It's your responsibility to see that your competition license and membership in the proper organizations are up to date, for instance. You should also know the schedule of events for the race, when the track will be open for practice and qualifying and when the drivers' meeting is going to be held. And you'd better be sure that your clock works right, too. I remember a race at Riverside a few years ago when Masten Gregory was driving a Lola but missed the start because daylight saving time had gone off that day, putting him an hour behind schedule. That might not have been the only reason, but Masten didn't drive that car very many races.

It's also important for you to study the supplemental regulations for each event. At some races a brief physical exam will be required even though your license is in effect and you've already had all the physicals you need. And almost every event has some little peculiarity that is different from every other event. In some races, for instance, the car is immediately disqualified if it goes behind the pit wall, while at others you can take the car back to the garage and work on it and still return to the race. As the driver, you need to be aware of all the special rules that pertain to the conduct of every event.

As a professional driver you will probably also find it necessary to have more personal driving equipment than was required when you were a club racer. When you were a club racer, for example, you were probably able to get along with one driving suit. As a professional you're certain to need at least two, and possibly more, depending on how much you are racing. In practical terms, there are times when you will really need to have a second suit ready for use. Once when I was driving a McLaren Can-Am car, it developed a fuel leak during the warm-up session before the race. The crew was able to stop the leak and because I had another suit in my bag I was able to change and avoid the irritation and burns I would have gotten if I had had to wear my fuel-soaked uniform.

A clean suit for the race is also important in another way. Public relations are an important part of the professional driver's life these days and it's pretty hard to make the right impression on a sponsor or a television audience if you look like you've been sleeping under the car all week.

PRACTICE & QUALIFYING

The principles of learning the course apply to both professional and club racing and since we've already covered these, I won't go over them again except to say that you should learn the course in the right sequence and learn it thoroughly.

Because most professional-category racing cars are so highly stressed and finely tuned, however, it's important not to use your car up during practice. As a club racer in a production category car you could probably stay on the track every minute that was available for practice and still not have enough time. As a professional driver in a racing car you should spend only as much time on the track as you honestly need. After you've learned the circuit and are ready to qualify, park the car and let the mechanics check it over to make sure it's ready for the qualifying session.

When it's time for qualifying, try to get out early. During qualifying sessions, almost all the drivers are pushing hard and as the session goes on it is almost inevitable that somebody will have a problem and put oil or coolant on the track, slowing everybody down. So try to get out when the track is still clean, do your best laps and then get off the course.

While you're out for qualifying, it's a good idea to pick your time for turning your fastest qualifying lap. Don't just try to go as fast as possible, lap after lap; that could cause you to overstress something that would hurt you later. If there's traffic in front of you, for instance, wait till it clears up before cranking on your hottest lap. You can't turn your fastest lap while working your way through other cars.

At some racing circuits, depending on where the timers are located, it is possible to use a special qualifying technique. The last turn before the timers is most important in this situation because you may be able to use it to your advantage. Coming up to what you want to be your fastest qualifying lap, treat the last turn before the timers as a Type I turn, even exaggerate it, and begin your acceleration just as early as possible to develop all possible speed to start the lap. Then, after putting together

your very best techniques all the way around the course, when you come to the last turn again, drive it as if it were a Type II turn. Here you keep all possible speed as long as you can, brake just as late as you can, and take the shortest line past the timing station. This technique doesn't make any significant difference in your lap time but it may be worth a couple tenths of a second and that just may be sufficient to move you up a position or two on the starting grid. And starting position is just as important in professional racing as it is in club racing. Maybe even more important, since some races pay off on starting positions as well as your position at the end.

After you've turned in an acceptable time, one in which you really believe you did everything about as well as possible, verify the fact that the officials have recorded this time and then save your car for the race.

THE RACE

For the race itself, it is important to have a game plan. What kind of race does the car owner or team manager want you to run? Some teams want you to charge from the very beginning and go just as fast as you can as long as the car will stay together while others will want you to take it very easy in the opening laps, stay out of trouble and then pick up the pace later. If it's a race where pit stops are required, a thorough understanding of every job should be worked out and practiced until everyone, including the driver, is expert at it. You may not think the driver has anything to do except drive in and stop but you'll find there's a lot more to it than that. You have to get into the pits just as quickly as possible, stop in a very precise area, communicate with the crew if there's something you have to tell them, and then get out again—all with the least loss of time. It's more of an art than you might think. Pit signals should also be understood by both you and the crew to make sure there's no confusion in the communication system.

If it's left up to you to decide how the race should be driven, you should tell your crew what you are planning. In most races, I think you should follow the same strategy as in a club race; that is, get the best start possible, pass everybody you can in the early laps, then see where you stand and decide what your strategy should be for the rest of the race. This is the time to settle down and work at turning good lap times while not taking any more out of the car than is necessary. Towards the end of the race, depending on how things are going, you may be able to move up to a better payoff in the standings or you may be able to ease off and still maintain your position.

Following the event it is important for you to pass along all the pertinent information that you have gained during the race. It's important to do this just as soon as practical after the race so it can be recorded and analyzed well in advance of the next event.

Driving as a professional can be very rewarding. It's much different than club racing, though, and has to be treated as such by most of us. Very few drivers who have raced as serious professionals ever come back to club racing even though they started there and thoroughly enjoyed club competition when they were in it. I'm not sure why this is but I would imagine it's because in professional racing the level of competition is generally better and also because it's far more glamorous. After having had a taste of the life of a professional racing driver, it isn't easy on the ego to go back to being just another club racer.

Last Lap

OKAY, that's about all there is to it. To start your career as a racing driver, you get a car, you prepare it and you go racing. I hope that all this has been of some help to you. What I have said in this book won't make you a winner automatically, but I think it can help make your career in competition driving a little easier because it does tell you some of the things you can expect to encounter in competition, and it also gives you some insight into how somebody else has approached the same problems. If you aren't aware of the possible pitfalls with which you will be faced, racing can be a very sad experience. On the other hand, if you approach it intelligently, staying within your limits—both those you encounter on the race track and those your bank balance will tell you about—it can be a tremendously rewarding experience. It has been for me and I hope it will be for you.

Good luck and good racing.

REFERENCES

Sports Car Club of America, P.O. Box 22476, Denver, Colo. 80222

International Motor Sports Association, Inc., P.O. Box 805, Fairfield, Conn. 06430

Automobile Competition Committee for the United States, FIA, Inc., 433 Vanderbilt Motor Parkway, Hauppauge, L.I., N.Y. 11787

United States Auto Club, 4910 West 16th St., Speedway, Ind. 46224

National Association of Stock Car Auto Racing, P.O. Box K, Daytona Beach, Fla. 32015

Jim Russell Racing Drivers School, P.O. Box 911, Rosamond, Calif. 93560

Bob Bondurant School of High Performance Driving, Ontario Motor Speedway, Ontario, Calif. 91761

Books

All But My Life, by Stirling Moss and Ken Purdy, E.P. Dutton & Co. Inc., New York, N.Y., 1963

From the Cockpit, by Bruce McLaren, Frederick Muller Ltd., London, England, 1964

Jim Clark, Portrait of a Great Driver edited by Graham Gauld, The Hamlyn Publishing Group Ltd., Middlesex, England, 1968

Life at The Limit, by Graham Hill, Coward-McCann, Inc., New York, N.Y., 1970

The Racing Driver, The Theory and Practice of Fast Driving, by Denis Jenkinson, Robert Bentley, Inc., Cambridge, Mass., 1964

The Technique of Motor Racing, by Piero Taruffi, Robert Bentley, Inc., Cambridge, Mass., 1958

Periodicals

Autosport, Haymarket Publishing Ltd., Gillow House, 5 Winsley St., London W.1, England, weekly magazine

Autoweek, Autoweek Building, Lafayette, Calif. 94549, weekly newspaper

Motoring News, Standard House, Bonhill St., London EC2, England, weekly newspaper

Road & Track, 1499 Monrovia Ave., Newport Beach, Calif. 92663, monthly magazine

---

EDITOR   Ed Reading

DESIGNER   Hal Crippen
ART ASSISTANT   Sonja Keith

PHOTOS   Gordon Chittenden, Bill Neale, Scott Malcolm, James T. Crow, Bill Warner, Alice Bixler, Jim Fisk.